Hamlyn all-colour paper backs

Reginald Hargreaves

Great Land Battles

Hamlyn · London
Sun Books · Melbourne

FOREWORD

It is difficult to refute Heraclitus' uncompromising pronunciamento that 'War is the father of all things', for no stage in the history of progress has been free from strife. Over and over again, even the most unbellicose of peoples have been driven to embark on warfare that they might live in peace.

It is not to applaud or even to condone warfare to manifest an interest in it. It is merely to accept it as an ineradicable human function, and at the same time to recognise that it can inspire the best in human nature as frequently as it can give rein to the worst.

The techniques of conflict have fully reflected mankind's expanding ingenuity. The handling and control of those entrusted with the actual task of waging war reveals progressive realisation of the fact that application of the relatively simple first principles of strategy is capable of infinite range and variety.

The great campaigns of history have invariably culminated in a decisive conflict from which one side or the other has emerged as the indubitable victor. It is with certain carefully selected encounters of this character that this volume is concerned.

R.H.

Published by the Hamlyn Publishing Group Limited
London · New York · Sydney · Toronto
Hamlyn House, Feltham, Middlesex, England
In association with Sun Books Pty Ltd, Melbourne

ISBN 0 600 33892 4
Phototypeset by BAS Printers Limited, Wallop, Hampshire
Colour separations by Schwitter Limited, Zurich
Printed in Holland by Smeets, Weert

CONTENTS

Hamlyn All Colour Paperbacks—Great Land Battles

Errata

For correct sequence of text read page 15 before page 14.

INTRODUCTION

Both peace and war are noble or ignoble according to their kind and occasion. *John Ruskin*

Conflict is as old as humanity itself. Since the days when the urge of some undernourished primordial tribe to seize the better-stocked hunting-grounds of a neighbour led to an exchange of blows, strife has been endemic in all ages. Indeed, it has been calculated that since 3,600 BC the world has known no more than 292 years that have been free from the clash of arms.

The craving for territorial expansion, dynastic rivalry, the friction arising from competing commerce, the race to exploit the new worlds brought into being by maritime enterprise, sectarian bigotry, even sheer racial antagonism – all these contingencies have offered endless opportunity for the various peoples to resort to strife in an attempt to resolve their differences.

At the outset both weapons and the tactics employed in their use were of the simplest, an occasional ambush forming the only alternative to a head-on rush to club the opponent out of action.

With mankind's discovery of the use of fire in the manipulation of metals, the fabrication of death-dealing implements divided them into two classes. There were 'shock' weapons – such as the sword, dagger, thrusting spear and axe – and 'missile' weapons – the sling, the javelin, or throwing spear, and then the bow: the light bow of the Persians, the English longbow, and the mechanised cross-bow so strongly favoured by the Genoese. With these went the protective armour of chain-mail and plate.

With the production of gunpowder and the consequent invention of manual firearms and then of cannon – passionately and justifiably represented as unwarrantably 'murtherous' by such contemporary paladins of 'chivalrous' warfare as the Florentine, Gian Paolo Vitelli, the *beau sabreur* Pierre du Terrail, and the *Chevalier sans peur et sans reproche*, the

Above, left: the medieval longbow. *Right*: a trebuchet – the medieval war engine for hurling missiles. *Below*: the crossbow.

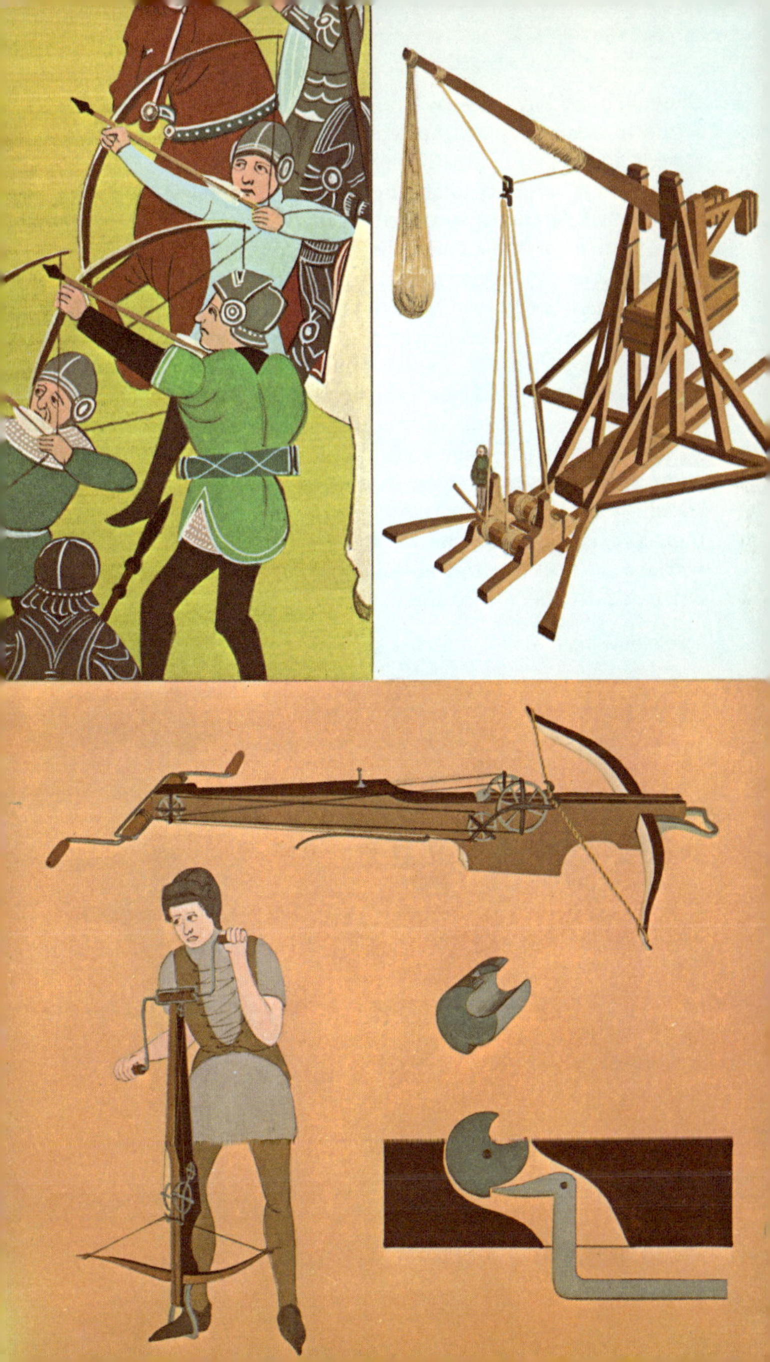

Chevalier de Bayard – warfare took on a new dimension: while in some respects becoming more deadly, at the same time it acquired far greater impersonality.

The first regular standing army, complete with the emperor's Life Guard, properly organised units and baggage train, and even the equivalent of army chaplains, was that of the ancient Assyrians. In Europe, after the collapse and extinction of the Roman Empire with its splendid legionaries, the first standing force was that inaugurated in 1454 by Charles VII of France, when fifteen companies of men-at-arms were given a fixed establishment.

But as the growth in populations extended warfare's scope, while at the same time the slow but steady improvement in firearms intensified its conduct, the need for regular standing forces became more and more self-evident. The time had come when the far more complicated conduct of warfare – both technical and tactical – could only be entrusted to the well-trained, completely organised profes-

A soldier using a triple-barrelled matchlock, *c.* 1505.

sional, somebody ready to take the field fully prepared to play his part in the fray from the very outset. For time is an unfriendly neutral on the side of the stronger; and improvisation not only adds enormously to the cost of war but gravely imperils its outcome. This is a grim fact of which democracies are ever in danger of losing sight. For it is extremely difficult to persuade a prosperously industrialised people snugly immersed in the congenial task of bettering their day-to-day standard of living to bear in mind that:

Plenty breeds Pride; Pride,
Envy;
Envy, Warre:
Warre, Poverty; Poverty
humble Care.
Humility breeds Peace and
Peace breeds Plenty.
Thus, round the World do
rowle alternately.

[Robert Hayman: *The World Whirliligge*]

'There is no substitute for victory', the late General Douglas MacArthur invariably insisted. But victory *per se* is not an event of particular moment, save to those whose skill, courage and

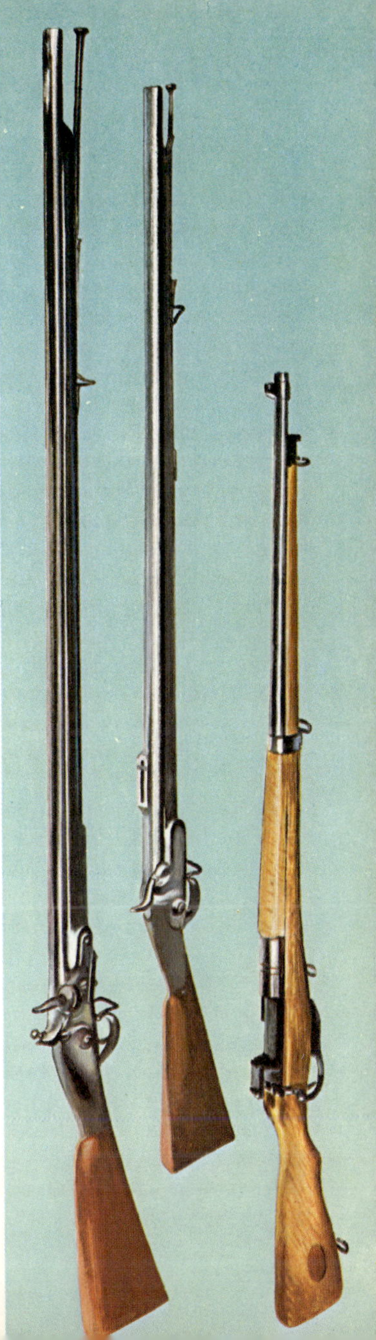

Left to right: musket, 1768; the Miniè, 1853; the Ross rifle, 1914.

endurance have brought it about. It is the *consequences* of victory, the political use that is made of it, that matters.

Napoleon, for example, scored an unquestionable victory over his Muscovite opponents in the Battle of Borodino. But Borodino was a veritable eunuch among victories since it bred nothing but frustration: the empty, meaningless occupation of Moscow and then the hounded retreat through the venomous winter snow and ice, involving the large-scale destruction and complete demoralisation of one of the most powerful forces ever to be mobilised.

Again, when in 1912 the Balkan League, made up of Serbia, Rumania, Bulgaria and Montenegro, secured an unquestionable victory over their Turkish opponents, so embittered was the dispute as to the best manner in which the said victory could be advantaged that in the end Serbia, Rumania and Montenegro combined to take the field against their recent co-adjutor, Bulgaria.

In these days, when the unrestricted curiosity of the scientists has culminated in the presentation to the world of the means of wholesale self-destruction, and humanity quakes under the doubtful restraint of 'the deterrent', we might justifiably exclaim:

Oh to go back a thousand years
When arrows winged their way,
When foemen fell upon the spears,
And swords were swung to slay!
Behold! Belching in Heaven black
Mushrooms obscene!
Dear God, the brave days give us back,
When wars were clean!

[*When Wars were Clean* (Anon.)]

In 1851 Sir Edward Creasy published his *Fifteen Decisive Battles of the World*. The bulk of the encounters described and analysed were of the classic Graeco-Roman period; and subsequent research has brought to light no further information regarding their conduct. Creasy also wrote of the battles of Hastings, Blenheim, Saratoga and Waterloo, with regard to which sufficient fresh material has come to light to warrant their careful reassessment. Hence their inclusion in the present volume.

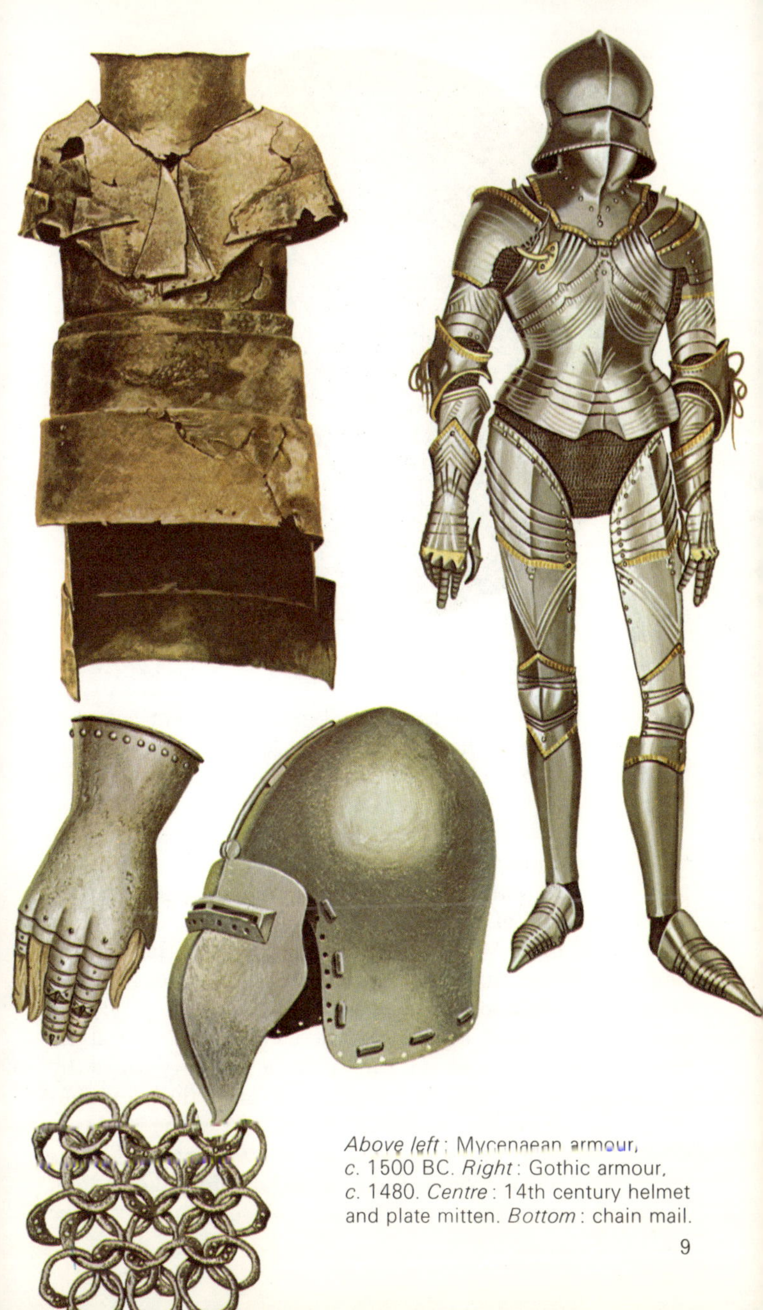

Above left: Mycenaean armour, *c*. 1500 BC. *Right*: Gothic armour, *c*. 1480. *Centre*: 14th century helmet and plate mitten. *Bottom*: chain mail.

Edward the Confessor.

HASTINGS 1066

With the death of England's well-intentioned but spineless monarch, Edward the Confessor, in January 1066, Harold Godwinson, Earl of Wessex, was anointed king by popular acclaim.

But Harold's accession to the throne had entirely failed to take into account the respective claims to the succession preferred by Tostig, the new incumbent's younger brother, and by William of Normandy.

So far as Duke William was concerned, it was his contention that on a visit to the Confessor's court in 1051 he had been given definite assurance that in due course England's governance would be his. Furthermore, in 1064 Harold, having been stranded on the coast of territory ruled by Count Guy of Ponthieu and imprisoned under the provisions of the 'law of wreck', had owed his release to the intervention of William of Normandy. It was while Harold was undergoing what amounted to a period of enforced detention as the Norman's 'guest' that he had been 'persuaded' to take an oath, on sacred relics, to support in due course Duke William's claim to the English throne. With the Confessor's death, however, Harold was at pains to make it clear that, because the pledge had been given under duress, it was entirely invalid and could be repudiated without fear of reproach.

The Norman's response was to set about the organisation of a body of experienced troops with which to support his claim to England's throne by force of arms.

But it was Tostig, abetted by Harald Hadrada, king of Norway, who was the first to throw down the gage; news of his landing in the Humber, at the head of a considerable body of troops, sent Harold racing northwards, together with his thanes and the pick of his men at arms.

At Stamford Bridge Harold hurled himself at the intruders in a successful foray in which both Tostig and Hadrada were slain and their followers driven into headlong retreat.

Meanwhile Duke William's preparations for invasion had suffered a serious setback, a sudden tempest having wrecked

Harold enthroned. From the Bayeux Tapestry.

a number of his ships along the coast between the Seine and the Orne. With a reconstituted armada assembled in the harbour at St Valèry, the wind – normally south-westerly – veered north-east, pinning the transports in their haven.

Actually, the delay, against which William railed so bitterly, worked out to his immeasurable advantage. By the end of the first week in September the men of the guardian fleet Harold had assembled at Sandwich had abandoned their vessels *en masse*, for 'the season of provisioning had begun, and no man could keep them there any longer'. In effect, lacking root crops to sustain their edible cattle throughout the winter, their owners slaughtered off and salted down the bulk of them to furnish day-to-day winter sustenance, a task to which every able-bodied man, including the seafarers, temporarily devoted all his energies.

Thus it was entirely unimpeded that Duke William made the passage of the narrow seas, heading his armament in the *Mora* – a gift from his wife, Matilda – at whose masthead fluttered the consecrated gonfanon (banner) which signalised that the enterprise had the sanction of Pope Alexander II. In the Norman's wake sailed a swarm of spoil-hungry adventurers from Poitou, Brittany, Flanders, Aquitaine and

William and Harold, after Harold's shipwreck.

The building of William's fleet.

Burgundy – men such as Renie of Fescamps, whose promised reward for having furnished a ship and a mere twenty men-at-arms was an English bishopric.

After a calm and entirely unchallenged passage, the duke and his supporters made their landing at Bulverhithe, between Pevensey and Hastings. The Duke, the last man to step ashore, stumbled and fell prostrate. A murmur of dismay instantly arose amongst the superstititous soldiery, which the duke as promptly quelled by leaping to his feet and extending his two hands full of sand. 'What now?' he exclaimed, 'what astonishes you? I have taken seizin of this land with my hands, and, by the splendour of God, as far as it extends it is mine, as it is yours.'

Their superstitious fears allayed, the troops immediately set about the occupation of Pevensey Castle and the erection of two wooden towers, brought over in sections, with which to strengthen the shallow bridge-head.

With close on 2,000 Horse and their chargers, plus some 5,000 Foot to maintain, the Duke's first concern was supplies. Thus instead of marching at once on Canterbury or London, much time had to be spent in rounding up desperately needed provender and forage.

apple tree' on its ridge. Just on a mile long and 150 yards broad, the Senlac position was joined to the main bulk of the Wealden Hills by a narrow isthmus with steep descents on either side; and on the summit of the position Harold fixed his two banners – the Dragon of Wessex, and his own Standard of the Fighting Man. As a defensive measure a breast-work of stakes and crossed woodwork, to halt the rush of enemy Horse, was erected behind a shallow ditch.

With advance posts thrown out to a considerable distance, Duke William could be in little doubt that his opponent proposed to challenge him, even if handicapped by numerically inferior forces. They were in singularly good heart – their camp echoed with laughter and song, as they filled and emptied their horn-cups, sprawled at their ease about their blazing fires. On his part Harold's spies reported that the opposing force was indeed formidable; but having entirely misread the function of the short-haired, clean-shaven Norman men-at-arms, solemnly averred that there were more priests in the Normans' camp than fighting-men in the whole English army! For the contemporary English

News of his Norman challenger's successful landing reached Harold while he was resting his troops at York. With the minimum of delay the Saxon leader and his immediate followers took the road southwards, the Northumbrian levies being directed to follow as speedily as possible.

Reaching London late on October 7, Harold remained there long enough to summon the levies of the neighbouring South Midland shires to join him. With a number of men – especially from the north – still to report for service, he set out on October 11 to confront the invader. A two-day forced march brought him to the outskirts of the Andredsweald, on the fringe of the district in which 'the Bastard' had already won control.

Harold took up a position at the point where the road from London to Hastings emerges from the woodlands and sets out to cross the open land bordering the coast. The chosen ground was the lonely hill overlooking the marshy valley-bottom of Senlac, and distinguished by 'the hoar

William in action. He captures the town of Dinant.

mode favoured luxuriant beards and moustaches, and a hair-length which helped to pad the scalp against the impact of the metal helmet in general use.

With the rival hosts confronting one another, a whole day was spent in fruitless negotiations. For to Duke William's demand that Harold either resign his crown in favour of the Norman, submit the matter of the succession to the arbitration of the Pope, or determine the issue by single combat, an entirely negative answer was resolutely returned.

Thus nothing was left but to resort to a trial at arms. With the Normans occupying a ridge opposite the English forces, with the dawn of Saturday, 14 October, Odo, Bishop of Bayeux and Duke William's half-brother, celebrated mass and then, mounting his war-horse, took a lance in hand and proceeded to marshal his body of Horse.

At the third hour of the day William launched his forces in three divisions against the English host on the heights. Ahead of the mass of Horse rode Taillefer, the minstrel, blithely throwing his sword in the air and catching it by the hilt, as he chanted the inspiring verses of the *Song of Roland*.

The bright morning sun, glinting on the Normans' and their allies' chain mail, kite shields and metal helmets, also

William I. From a statue in Wells Cathedral.

Norman soldiers. From a medieval MS.

brought to gaudy life their surcoats of silk, embroidered or painted with the heraldic devices by which the riders were individually distinguished.

Attacking from three different sides, the task entrusted to the right wing was to assail and seek to outflank their opponents' left. Deploying to the right from the road, the assault force speedily discovered that, having wound around the eastern spur of the hill, the farther slopes were so steep as to be unassailable by mail-clad infantry, let alone by more heavily-accoutred men on horseback. The left wing was confronted with an even harder task, demanding a circuitous flank march up and across hindering broken ground, with a jutting knoll or hillock barring the way to the western spur of the battlefield. Only in the centre was there a fairly even gradient up to the plateau upon which the English force had taken its stand.

Protected by their stockade and shallow ditch, the English

had formed a shield-wall, with the house-carls occupying the most vulnerable position in the left centre. They were equipped with axes, swords, spears and javelins, the first-named being unquestionably the most favoured, but of missile weapons, such as the bow carried by a number of their opponents, they had little knowledge or experience. On the flanks a swarm of rustics, crudely armed with a few spears, clubs, billhooks and even sickles, sent out their skirmishers to challenge some of the Norman Foot who were probing cautiously forward. It was in the course of these preliminary sallies that Taillefer, having cut down a couple of his opponents, was brought crashing from his saddle, overcome by the swarm of assailants who pressed about him, and it is scarcely in question that his downfall had an extremely demoralising effect on the Normans, who had long regarded him as a veritable talisman of victory.

It was under cover of a flight of arrows that Duke William loosed his armoured Horse at the shield-wall of the English left-centre, where

Norman cavalry and, above, archers. From the Bayeux Tapestry.

the pick of Harold's house-carls was massed behind stockades. Baulked by the strength of the breastwork, many of the knights flung themselves from their saddles and sought desperately to tear the stout wooden stakes from the ground, only to be beaten back by a rain of blows from the two-handed Saxon axes and battered by the torrent of javelins and stone-headed hammers hurled at them at close range.

The first sign of wavering came from the Breton contingent on the assailants' left. Clubbed, hewn and mercilessly hammered, they stumbled into confusion and retreat. Unable to resist the temptation, a number of the English broke rank to chase their enemies down the hill, driving many of them into the little purling brook running along the low ground at the foot of the slope. The disorder quickly extended to the Norman centre, and gradually the whole line fell back. In the general confusion Duke William was unhorsed, and the cry went up that he was slain.

Flinging himself across the line of fugitives, Bishop Odo tried bravely to arrest their flight; while Duke William, springing back into the saddle, hastened to his kinsman's support. Throwing back his helmet, he cried out in a great voice, 'Here I am, alive; and please God we shall win yet!'

With the Normans and their allies rallying and again under control, the English of the right wing, who had rashly ventured from their position on the crown of the hill, were surrounded and cut down almost to a man.

Reorganised and reanimated by their leader's high-hearted determination to get the better of his opponents' stubborn resistance, the main Norman host again essayed an all-out assault on the 'linden wall' – that combination of shields and defensive stakes made from the wood of the linden tree, which no weapon was capable of splintering.

But the second onrush of the Norman Horse and Foot met with no greater measure of success than had the first. A few gaps were bludgeoned in 'the wall', but they were quickly closed again, and the few assailants who had successfully managed to penetrate it were either hurled out again or stayed within it at the cost of their lives.

For one signal advantage of the English position was that

The Normans charge the Saxon remnant.

the Norman archers had nothing to aim at but the shields of the front rank of their opponents, the men in the rear ranks being fully covered by them and out of sight.

It was at this juncture that Duke William, finding that sheer valour had failed to bring about the desired result, had recourse to guile. A feint at withdrawal had the hoped-for result of enticing the English into impetuous pursuit. But when the Normans rounded on them, yet again they withdrew in sufficiently good order to take up position once more behind their battered stockade.

By this time both sides had fought themselves into a state not far removed from complete exhaustion. But, undeterred by the setbacks he had so far experienced, William quietly gave orders for his bowmen to aim their shafts over the heads of their opponents' front-rank men, so as to allow the arrows to fall on the masses in the rear. At the same time the Horse and Foot pressed steadily forward under cover of the high-angle barrage.

The curving, dropping arrows were something neither the thanes nor the men of the fyrd had ever previously encountered, and they were utterly at a loss how best to deal with this hail of missiles that struck at an angle which rendered defence wellnigh impossible. 'Helmets were pierced, eyes were put out; men strove to guard their heads with their shields, and, in so doing, they were of course less able to wield their axes.'

Thus, at last, the shield wall fell into disarray; and it was at this vital moment that a drop-arrow pierced Harold's right eyeball, and though with an effort he wrenched it out, the report of the wound circulated at once amongst his dwindling band of followers, spreading immediate alarm and despondency. With the sun already sinking, many of the raw shire-levies began to slink off into the darkening forest so invitingly close to the hilltop shambles.

The ring of house-carls round the stricken Harold was shrinking fast. Yet, while the Norman Horse took up the pursuit of the fugitives in the nearby forest, the remnant of the thanes and men of the bodyguard doggedly kept up the fight, although they were so closely hemmed in that the dead had scarcely room to fall. One stalwart thane clove the skull of a Norman's charger in two with a single blow before himself being struck down by Roger de Montgomeri's lance.

But as twilight deepened a band of Norman knights closed in on the sorely wounded Harold as he bent, bleeding, over his shield, and ruthlessly hacked him to death.

As darkness fell the Saxon chieftain and the Wessex thanes who had so loyally supported him lay dead in a ring beneath the fluttering papal gonfalon, with which the Norman victors had speedily replaced the drooping banner of the Saxon Fighting Man. Belated reinforcements, making their way towards the coast, immediately turned back upon encountering the fugitives fleeing through the woods.

The duke followed up his victory with the absolute minimum of delay. Dover Castle having been secured as a base, he promptly set out across the Kentish downs, heading for the capital. Small as his force was, the resistance he encountered was no more than trifling.

Having crossed the Thames at Wallingford, the Duke – like Caesar before him – struck eastwards to cut off the capital from the north. With no help forthcoming from the Earls of Mercia and Northumbria, the dispirited Londoners hastened to send envoys to the Duke's headquarters at Berkhamstead to parley for terms. Unequivocal as they proved to be, there was no hope of successfully questioning them; and thus, on Christmas Day, in the abbey of Westminster, the illegitimate offspring of Robert III, Duke of Normandy, and Arletta, the daughter of a humble tanner of Falaise, was duly crowned King of England.

It was in no sense an easy heritage. A few thousand knights and men-at-arms had conquered a nation of stout fighters, skilled craftsmen and industrious husbandmen, with a genius for managing their local affairs which had consolidated in the admirable administration of shire and village.

Committed as he might be to rewarding those who had supported him in his initial venture, the new king still sought to enlist the aid of those English lords and prelates who had reconciled themselves to the fact that he sat on the throne by right of conquest.

Confiscation of lands was confined to the demesnes of those who had actually fought against him; although anything in the nature of an insurrection to overthrow his rule was suppressed with terrifying severity.

Yet even if he did ultimately succeed in transferring the ownership of virtually every large estate from English to Norman hands, at least it cannot be denied that he completely reorganized the country's measures of defence and put them on a thoroughly sound footing, while at the same time establishing a condition of law and order which enabled the contemporary chronicler, Wace, to affirm that 'a man that was worth aught might travel over the Kingdom with his bosom full of gold unhurt'.

From sharing in the gradual decline which overtook the North, England was brought within the orbit of the Mediterranean and all the immeasurable opportunities for commercial and cultural advancement of which succeeding generations took such profitable advantage. It was indeed not without significant influence on the future that 'the Normans high-mettled the blood in the English veins'.

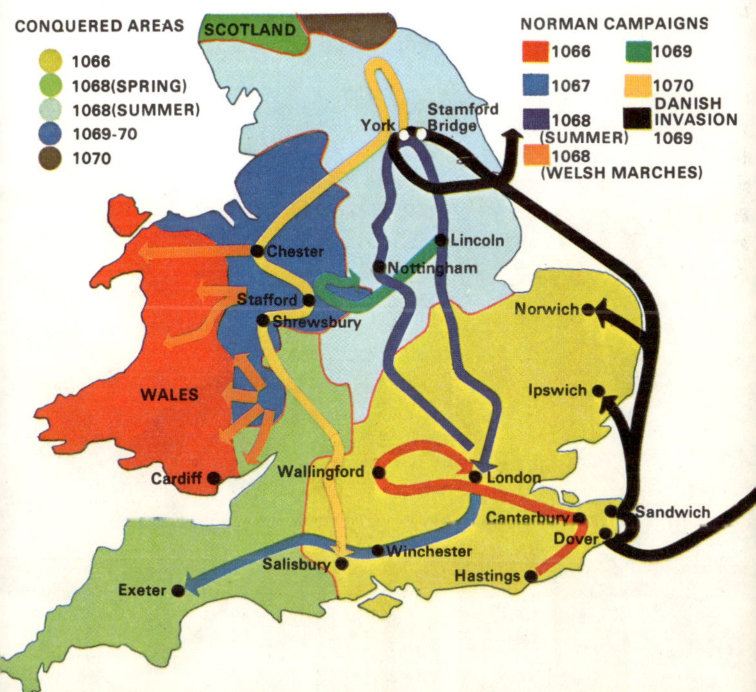

CONSTANTINOPLE

For centuries the European peoples fought desperately to repel the 'barbarians' – Assyrians, Avars, Persians, Carthaginians, Saracens, Moors and Turcomen – who sought to invade and take possession of their Western opponents' homelands. With the upsurge of the Islamic faith religious intolerance increased existing racial antagonism.

The collapse of the 'counter-offensive' of the Crusades resulting from Saladin's overwhelming victory of Hattin, in AD 1187, led to a renewed ascendancy of the Islamic world. It was a development which Europe was dangerously inclined to underrate owing to her preoccupation with the Hundred Years' War, the quarrel between France and the Church – which was no more than temporarily modulated in AD 1305 by the elevation of a Frenchman, Clement V, to the papal throne – and the first serious outbreak of the Black Death, which ultimately robbed the Continent of nearly half its population.

The Fourth Crusade (AD 1200–5), while temporarily sweeping back the hordes of Islam, had in the process

Mahomet at the siege of Banu Nadir. From a Persian MS.
Right: Murad I.

ravaged Constantinople and left it prostrate.

Unhappily it was at this juncture that Europe's Eastern Empire witnessed the supercession of the Latin peoples by the Byzantine Greeks. With Constantinople their immediate concern and responsibility, an era of degeneracy, of enervating pastimes and abstract polemical discussion characterized a population whose first concern should have been to harden and prepare itself for a renewal of the struggle with Islam, which obviously could not be long delayed.

For in the first half of the fifteenth century the Turkish victory in the second battle of Kossovo in October 1448 left the 'barbarian' invaders firmly established in Adrianople, with the Bulgarians and Hungarians cowering behind their frontiers, and Constantinople, thrust like a finger between two temporarily parted rows of teeth, virtually at the mercy of any Turkish force really determined upon its capture.

Then in February 1451 Murad (or Amurath) II, Sultan of Turkey, breathed his last, to be succeeded by his headstrong son, Mahomet II. The new ruler immediately gave the world a grimly illuminating taste of his quality: speeding to Adrianople, he first ensured the issue of the succession by drowning his infant brother, thereafter peremptorily marrying off his mother to a slave.

Almost from childhood it had been Mahomet's prime ambition to wrest the proud and stately city of Constantinople from the hands of the 'unbelievers', a fact of which its ruler, Constantine XI, was perfectly well aware, while being entirely unable to persuade his effete and debilitated people to take any of the necessary measures of precaution. Neither, with war clouds threatening the Byzantine Empire, could much in the way of help be looked for from other realms. The king of Catalonia, like Hunyadi the Hungarian, haggled and baulked. Frederick of Austria talked a lot but did nothing. Genoa and Venice promised thirty fully-armed galleys, but initially all that actually put in an appearance added up to one braying cardinal and 200 men-at-arms. It was at this juncture that the Genoese colony established at Galata (Pera), the suburb of Constantinople north of the Golden Horn, elected to pronounce its unqualified neutrality.

With the narrowest stretch of the Bosphorous commanded by recently erected twin forts, Mahomet hastened to marshal his strength for the task of reducing a city which, when manned by a resolute garrison, could rank as one of the

Constantinople, from a medieval MS. *Right*: Mahomet II.

most formidable strongholds in the world.

Facing the land approaches from Adrianople, the metropolis was defended by a triple enclosing wall, overlooking a deep ditch some five miles in length. The first wall was commanded by the second, and the second by the third, each overtopping the line of defence below it, all three being liberally equipped with military engines capable of playing on the siege works of a beleaguering army. Loopholes at a level below the battlements enabled the garrison to fire from a second line of well-protected apertures.

Opposite the Sea of Marmara the fortifications were virtually inaccessible and therefore unassailable. Across the mouth of the Golden Horn an enormous chain denied access to the long, narrow inlet beyond, in which Constantine's fleet of nine galleys and thirty guard boats had taken refuge.

The land wall was pierced by nine gates, of which the most important were the Xylo Porta, the Adrianople Gate, the central Gate of St Romanus, and the Golden Gate. Water supply was ensured by the Lycus stream, which flowed into the city, and whose damming Mohomet was completely to overlook. To man these extensive works Constantine could

count on no more than 5,000 native-born defenders out of a population of 100,000. Auxiliary contingents of Venetians, Genoese and Cretans added a further 3,000 to the garrison, command of which was entrusted to the veteran Genoese *condottiere*, John Justiniani.

Against these pitifully inadequate defence forces Mahomet could marshal an army of 165,000, headed by 15,000 well trained and firmly disciplined janissaries. But it was in his artillery train that the sultan placed his greatest confidence, the Wallachian cannon-founder Urban having furnished him with a number of monster brass pieces propelling stone cannon-balls weighing up to 150 pounds. At the head of this formidable armament, Mahomet took up his station beneath the city's walls on the fifth day of the April of 1453.

With a fleet numbering up to 350 vessels blockading the city from the Sea of Marmara, the heavy pieces of ordnance were dragged into place. Then amidst wild shouts of jubilation, the fervent prayers of the *imams*, and the frenzied beating of drums, the first major bombardment in history opened up with a vivid spurt of flame and the roaring detonation of Urban's gargantuan siege guns.

After fourteen days' steady battering of the city's walls, Mahomet judged the time ripe to essay his first general assault. Concurrently with this landward attack an attempt would be made to destroy the boom and chain defending the entrance to the Golden Horn.

As night set in on 18 April the onslaught was duly launched, a wild rush of Bashi-Bazouks scrambling into the ditch, their dead and wounded bodies serving as a bridge to aid the crossing of the janissaries, who bore the main burden of the attack. Archers and cavalrymen, fighting on foot, also joined in the turmoil that raged about the walls. But the tremendous fire of arquebuses, bows, cross-bows, catapults and wall-guns with which Justiniani and his followers immediately opened up broke the assailants' onrush on the barrier of their own killed and wounded.

Hearing that the attack on the boom had also misfired, Mahomet gave the word for the assault on the city walls to be halted. Sullenly but still defiantly the assailants drew off; and so infuriated was their leader by his setback that his henchmen had the greatest difficulty in dissuading him from loading his trebuchets with the corpses of the slain and firing them at such an angle as would ensure that the bodies fell within the walls, with every possibility of thus generating an outbreak of pestilence.

Still smarting at his failure to rush Constantinople's landward defences, Mahomet next had the mortification of witnessing a severe reverse inflicted on his fleet by three powerful Genoese warships, which arrived in local waters as escort to a merchant vessel loaded with grain.

As the craft completed their passage through the Dardanelles and approached the waters near the capital, they were promptly set upon by a swarm of Turkish vessels, much frailer in build, but, as one anxious onlooker on the city's walls observed, 'complete with men who intended to win'.

However the wind freshening in their favour, the far heavier Genoese vessels crashed their way through their lighter-draught opponents, stoving in the sides of the Turkish galleys, and shearing away the lengthy sweeps by

Janissaries. *Left to right*: lancer, quartermaster, and cavalryman with pike.

A mounted Egyptian lancer of Mahomet II's army. *Right*: Turkish bombardiers.

which they were propelled. Then, as the Muslim seamen sought to board and enter, pots of reeking 'Greek Fire' and a rain of stones, darts, javelins and arrows beat down mercilessly on the assailants' close-pressed ranks, while the swivel pieces swept their decks with a hail of small-shot, and axemen swept away the few venturesome boarders who had contrived to secure a precarious hand-hold.

For two full hours the conflict swung to and fro, and throughout the whole of it Mahomet, galloping his horse almost into the surf, bellowed his demand for victory and the ruthless extirpation of the 'accursed Unbelievers'.

The four Genoese vessels continued to force a passage for themselves until, with the lowering of the boom at Seraglio Point, they passed safely into the haven of the Golden Horn.

It was at this juncture that Mahomet conceived the fantastic project of seizing the Golden Horn by transporting a fleet of light-draught vessels *overland* across the Galata peninsula and re-launching them in the upper reaches of the haven, opposite the Xylo Porta. Timber to furnish ships' cradles and to construct a corduroy track and slipway nearly ten miles in length was secretly assembled; and by late April the means of passage had been completed. Then with cables, cradles and rollers manned by sweating slaves and patient bullocks, the trackway itself slippery with the grease of slaughtered sheep and oxen, some eighty craft were hauled from the water and sent lumbering on their way to be re-launched in the upper waters of the inlet, west of Galata.

A Greek attack on these vessels ended in crushing failure; nor was any serious attempt made to impede Mahomet's construction of a barrel bridge across the top of the Horn. This bridge, 2,000 feet in length and with a central fairway eight feet wide, served to link the two wings of the Islamic army, and establish an additional artillery position from which the bombardment of the walls could be appreciably intensified.

A steady cannonade of the city was followed, early in May, by further massed assaults, mainly directed at the sector around the St Romanus Gate. On both occasions the assailants were beaten back, with enormous losses, by Justiniani and the more stalwart of the defenders.

But Mahomet's losses, considerable as they were, had been more than made good by the fresh contingents sum-

moned to his banner. Yet the very fact that he was thus enabled to maintain the number of troops under command posed in itself a problem whose solution could not be deferred indefinitely. For with so many mouths to feed, the sources of supply soon seemed likely to become exhausted, and it emerged only too clearly that unless the city could be taken by the end of the month, the siege would have to be abandoned for sheer want of provisions to feed the besiegers.

Finding that for all his efforts he could not entirely deter Constantinople's garrison from repairing the city's battered walls, Mahomet resolved that his next attempt to storm them should be made under the protection of a *helepolis* or 'city-taker'. This was a huge but mobile wooden tower, with platforms, brows, scaling ladders and its own self-contained artillery, which with furious energy was wheeled forward until it overhung a breach in the wall that still awaited repair.

From this vantage point the Turks flung down into the ditch huge stones, fascines and even the rubble of the battered rampart itself, with the idea of making a rough-and-ready causeway for the passage of their main assault forces.

From daylight to sunset the conflict raged with unabated fury, with Justiniani and the pick of his followers tirelessly battling to hurl back wave after wave of assailants regardless of the cost to their own thinning ranks. With the last onrush beaten off, the intrepid *condottière heaved a number of* barrels of gunpowder into the ditch and, setting fire to the brushwood with which it had become choked, succeeded in blowing the *helepolis* into splinters.

All attempts to take the city by open assault having so far been repelled, resort was next made to sapping and mining, mainly in the vicinity of the Kaligaria and Adrianople Gates. For ten days every effort was made to undermine the walls; but in every instance the attempt was frustrated by counter-mining. In the event, the Turks were either drowned by flooding in their underground galleries by the waters of the Lycus stream, smoked out by the suffocating reek of

The siege at its height.

stink-pots, tackled in close-combat with axe, spear and dagger, or blown up by camouflets which exploded 'with a great crash so that a greenish whirlwind carried the Turks in the air, so that fragments of men and timber fell in the city and into the camp'.

It is possible that in this moment of deflation Mahomet might have been prepared to lift the siege, had not his chief subordinate, Zagan Pasha, taken occasion to remind his overlord that Alexander the Great, with an army in no way comparable in size to the host commanded by the sultan, had conquered, not merely a single city, but a whole world. With this the outraged monarch swore by the most sacred of oaths that he would bring Constantinople crawling to submission or perish in the attempt.

For what he had determined should be his final and triumphant assault, Mahomet chose three main points of attack, of which the onslaught on the St Romanus Gate sector was to be the point of decision. With a garrison known to have been reduced to a bare 4,000 effectives, it was calculated that a triple offensive would so dangerously disperse the defence that at no point would it be strong enough to repel attack.

Worked up to a frenzy of enthusiasm by the promise of double pay and three days' unrestricted licence once the city had fallen into their hands, on the morning of 29 May the Turkish forces – 10,000 janissaries, and 250,000 Bashi-Bazouks, Anatolians, Kurds and Dervish hirelings – hurled themselves at the quaking capital.

The foremost ranks were made up of a rabble of loot-hungry freebooters, lusting for the pillage which would be theirs once the defence had been overcome. Spurred on by the thought of the spoil that victory would bring them 'the common impulse drove them onwards to the wall; the most audacious to climb were instantly destroyed; and not a dart, not a bullet of the defenders was idly wasted on the accumulated throng. But their strength and ammunition were exhausted in this laborious defence; the ditch was filled with the bodies of the slain; they supported the

The Turks victorious.

footsteps of their companions; and of this desperate vanguard, the death was more serviceable than the life'.

It was the task of the more seasoned janissaries to make good the advantage won by the preliminary assault of the irregulars, and in steady, disciplined ranks they swung into action, with the Greeks, headed by Constantine himself, seeking desperately to consolidate their defence. But the janissaries surged irresistibly forward, tearing aside the stout stockade by which the portals had hopefully been strengthened.

It was the neglect to maintain a sufficient guard over the postern of the Kerkoporta – or Circus Gate, a mere half-mile away from where Justiniani and the pick of his men battled with the onslaught's main thrust – which brought quickening ruin on the defence. For a party of janissaries, having forced the portal, made their way along the inner enclosure to take the defenders unexpectedly in flank. Their sudden intervention created such bewildering confusion that their comrades at the St Romanus Gate were enabled to storm their way into the city in ever-increasing numbers.

It was at this critical juncture that Justiniani was struck down, so sorely hurt that he had to be borne away from the scene of conflict.

One last desperate attempt to stem the surging tide of Turkish victory was headed by Constantine himself. 'God forbid', he swore, 'that I should live an Emperor without an Empire. As my city falls, I will fall with it.' These words had scarcely left his lips before he was ruthlessly cut down, wounded without hope of recovery.

With the death of Constantine in this last, decisive action, all attempts at organised resistance dissolved in a veritable orgy of slaughter. Men, women and children by the thousand were the victims of insensate massacre; hundreds of would-be fugitives were trampled to death at the gates. Houses were pillaged, and their inhabitants slain; while the scores seeking refuge in the Church of St Sophia were mercilessly cut down or set aside to serve as slaves.

With sadistic self-indulgence, Mahomet then amused himself by purchasing from his followers such of the leading

Greek noblemen as had fallen into their hands, thereafter having them ceremoniously executed in his presence.

The shock which swept the Western world with the news of Constantinople's fall was nowhere felt more acutely than in the Vatican. Rome had failed to save one of her children, and thus tremendous impetus was given to that wave of doctrinal dissension which was to culminate in the schismatic revolt of Martin Luther and the proselytes of the Reformation.

As the historian Gelzer dispassionately summed up the situation resulting from Constantinople's fall: 'The month of May 1453 had dragged the Byzantine Empire finally to its grave. The Greek supremacy had long been a thing of the past; the hollow phantom of it was now to vanish away.'

In effect, the stage was set for the rise of the more virile peoples of north-western Europe, with all the expansion and international friction that were to be the inevitable accompaniment of that development.

An early cannon. From *Chronique d'Angleterre,* 1480.

BLENHEIM 1704

It was at the invitation of a Whig junta headed by the Earl of Orford that Queen Mary's consort, William of Orange, took the throne as reigning monarch. Once installed, he lost no time in committing Britain to the support of Holland in her desperate struggle to stave off conquest by the French.

The ensuing six years of arduous campaigning, while demonstrating the British soldier's admirable fighting quality, did little to enhance William's reputation as a commander in the field. So in 1697, with both sides wellnigh exhausted, hostilities were temporarily halted by the conclusion of the extremely brittle Peace of Ryswick.

Immediately, with incredible lack of foresight, the British parliament insisted upon the reduction of the standing army from a strength of 87,000 to a mere cadre of 30,000.

Fortunately, the blundering of Britain's enemy served to spare her the just consequences of her folly. For in 1701 the throne of Spain, having fallen vacant, was left by testamentary decree to Philip, the grandson of Louis XIV of France. Such an immense accretion of power as this implied, to an individual whose aim was nothing less than the hegemony of Europe, was clearly not to be tolerated. Without a moment's hesitation Sweden, Prussia, Denmark, Holland and the Austrian Empire formed an anti-French alliance, to which England proffered her unqualified support when Louis, on the death of William III, gave open recognition to the exiled Jacobite claimant of the throne.

Immediate steps were taken to increase the British army's strength to 40,000. For the French forces had opened the campaign by securing the whole of the Spanish Netherlands, with its many fortresses, and under the command of Marshal Boufflers had concentrated near Cleve, poised for a direct descent on Holland.

Command of the first contingent of 18,000 British troops assigned to Flanders was entrusted to John Churchill, Earl – subsequently Duke – of Marlborough. Service in Tangier, at sea in the battle of Solebay of 1672, and under the veteran Turenne, had clearly demonstrated his innate genius for war, given anything like a free hand. Unhappily, though theoretically in supreme command of the Allies as well as of the British contingent, he was anything but a free agent, the Dutch having attached to their forces certain civilian 'field deputies' whose prime concern was to ensure the welfare and safety of their own troops, even to the point of

Louis XIV.

exercising an absolute veto on their charges' participation in an imminent battle.

Thus at the very outset of operations Marlborough's promising strategy was twice almost completely stultified by the Dutch 'dragging their feet'. It was only the British leader's steadfast resolve to accomplish something of outstanding value to the campaign – Dutch or no Dutch – which resulted in his capture of Venlo, Ruremonde and Liège – no mean outcome to a year's hard fighting, despite the failure to inflict wholesale defeat on the French field army and that of their ally, Maximilian of Bavaria.

Throughout the following year it was Marlborough's chief aim to keep the main French army under Marshal Villeroi pinned down on the Meuse, while Antwerp and Ostend were laid under siege and the British fleet threatened a landing at Dieppe.

But Marshal Villars had entered Bavaria to join hands with Maximilian, obviously with the aim of imposing a crushing defeat on the Imperial Austrian troops, to open up the way for a direct descent on Vienna, whose fall would inevitably lead to the dissolution of the Grand Alliance.

Bavaria was thus the obvious key to the situation; and Marlborough's apparently insoluble problem was how to unite with the Emperor's forces on the Danube without abandoning to the Dutch the sole defence of their frontier, a responsibility they were as unwilling to assume as they were incapable of fulfilling with any degree of efficiency.

At the beginning of 1704 the initial suggestion was for a campaign on the Moselle, with the ultimate object of marching on Paris, a project to which the Dutch assented with considerable reluctance.

But to the amazement of friend and foe alike, Marlborough, at the head of an army of 50,000, suddenly swung south-eastwards into Germany. Despite bad roads and the foulest of weather, in less than six weeks the Duke's men had covered the 250 miles to the Danube and were concentrated near Ulm, their unlooked-for appearance on the flank and rear of the Franco-Bavarian forces putting an immediate end to

Left: John Churchill in the Foot Guards, aged 18. *Below, left*: Marlborough, after Godfrey Kneller. *Right*: the Earl of Godolphin.

any designs they may have entertained for a descent on Vienna. At this juncture, as the Prince of Baden marched off his troops for the investment of Ingoldstadt, that Marlborough was joined by a force of 4,000 Imperialists, headed by Prince Eugene of Savoy, a leader whose military talents were second only to those of Marlborough himself.

The key to the Elector's capital of Munich was the bridge over the Danube at Donauwerth, covered by the Schellenberg, a commanding eminence which the Franco-Bavarians hastily started to put in a state of defence. Marlborough thereupon decided to attack forthwith before the position could be fully fortified.

Subsequent to a gruelling fifteen-mile approach march, the Duke hurled his British infantry against the key position on the Schellenberg, and after an hour and a half of bitter fighting the height was won, with the beaten enemy withdrawing southwards towards Augsburg. There they were compelled to look on impotently as the Allied armies systematically laid waste the fruitful territory of Bavaria in the hope of forcing the Elector to sue for terms. This hope was soon dashed, however, when Maximilian was joined by Marshal Tallard at the head of a large body of French.

For the moment Marlborough found himself confronted by an army which, totalling 60,000, with 120 guns and mortars, was numerically far superior to his own. For even when he had crossed the Danube to link up with Prince Eugene and his Imperialists, their joint force comprised a total of a little under 50,000, supported by no more than 60 pieces of artillery.

The Franco-Bavarian host was less than five miles distant at Blenheim, on the north bank of the Danube, between Dilligen and Donauwerth. It was a position that Tallard was supremely confident his opponents would find far too strong to attack. In this the Frenchman had underrated the steely resolution of his principal opponent. 'I know the difficulties', the Duke retorted to those who urged on him the dangers inherent in launching an assault, 'but a battle is absolutely necessary; and I rely on the discipline of my troops.'

A careful reconnaissance revealed that the terrain between

Prince Eugene of Savoy.

Marshal Tallard.

the two camps consisted of a plain of varying breadth stretching between the Danube and a chain of woodlands, with the Franco-Bavarian camp lying to the west. The plain was intersected by a number of streams running down at right angles to the Danube, no less than three of which crossed the obvious line of march between the Anglo-Imperialist camp and the position taken up by Tallard. This was behind the marshy Nebel brook, between the village of Blenheim and the hamlet of Lutzingen. With the Frenchman's right wing resting on the Danube and his left reasonably well secured by hilly and thickly wooded country, Blenheim itself was defended by the pick of the French infantry, with the cavalry disposed so as to hold the centre of the line, and the Elector of Bavaria's troops entrusted with the maintenance of resistance on the left.

Marlborough's original plan was to swiftly carry the village of Blenheim, turn the French right and cut them off from any potential help forthcoming from Hochstadt, their support centre some two and a half miles in rear.

But the morning of 13 August was misty, and in any case the Duke had to delay his primary assault until Prince Eugene, on the right wing, with extremely difficult terrain to traverse, had got his forces into position.

The stone bridge over the Nebel, taking the road from Hochstadt by way of Blenheim to Donauwerth, had been partly broken down, and while waiting for Eugene's deployment to be completed, the Duke had this repaired. At the same time five pontoon bridges were thrown across the water; although the stream itself was scarcely more of an obstacle than the treacherous marshy ground on either side.

It was not until 12.30 p.m. that Eugene could report that he was ready to attack and, the artillery having opened fire, Marlborough proceeded to ride down the whole length of the line in full view of his troops. At one point a round shot struck the ground right under his horse, temporarily obscuring both steed and rider in a swirling cloud of dust. A gasp of horror went up from the onlooking troops,

The route of Marlborough's march.

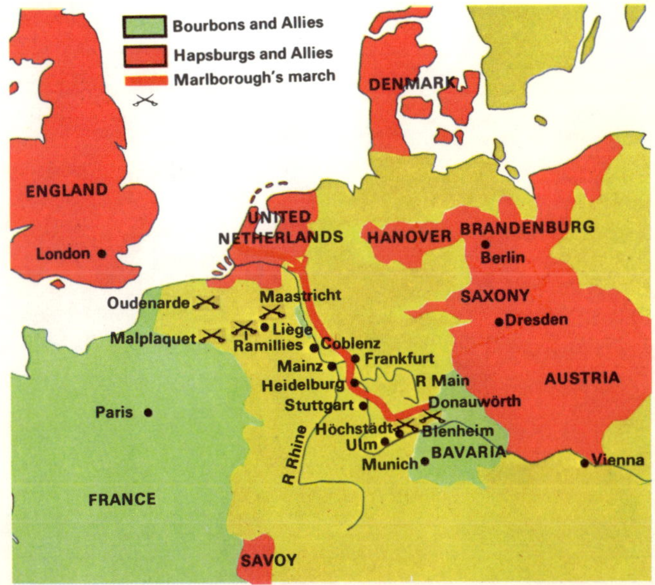

which turned into a babble of relief as the dust cleared and the well-loved figure of 'Corporal John' was seen, in his scarlet coat and blue ribbon of the Garter, calmly brushing himself down as he continued his unhurried progress along the line.

Owing to the hampering mist and the delays Eugene had suffered in taking up his position, Tallard had been given ample time in which to make his dispositions, to concentrate the cream of the Gallic infantry in Blenheim village and to support them by entrenching a body of dragoons behind a waggon-leaguer on the nearby river bank; while his subordinate, Marsin, together with the Elector, was solidly drawn up on the left wing.

With Eugene at last in a position to bear his part in the fray, the time had come to launch the attack on the vital position of Blenheim. Headed by 'Salamander' Cutts – so named in tribute to his abnormal 'taste for fire' – the

Marlborough and his staff. Beyond, the armies move into position.

infantry moved into position in six lines. The order had been given that not a shot was to be fired until the brigadier leading the first line had reached the palisades hastily erected for the village's defence, and had thrust his sword into the timber as a sign that abandonment of the blade was in no circumstances to be condoned. On the right of Cutt's division, four cavalry regiments also moved up, while the balance of the troops advanced towards the Nebel in four-line formation with the guns roaring into action on the higher ground to their rear. A detached body was entrusted with the task of ensuring that the force attacking Blenheim should not be assailed on flank and rear by enemy troops debouching from Oberglau, the village a couple of miles to the east of Blenheim.

Under a heavy fire of grape-shot Cutts's division made the difficult crossing of the Nebel stream to advance resolutely on Blenheim. At thirty paces distance they were received by a deadly fire; but there was no reply since Brigadier Row had given orders that the village must be carried by

the bayonet. Pressing doggedly forward, true to his promise the Brigadier thrust his sword into the palisades, and his men, after pouring in a single volley, rushed forward, striving to drag down the pales by sheer bodily strength, in a desperate effort to force an entrance. But with Row mortally wounded and a third of his brigade put out of action, the whole force fell back in considerable disorder. While still in a state of temporary confusion they were charged by three squadrons of Gendarmes, one of whom seized the colours of the Twenty-first, which were only retrieved when, pursuing their advance too far, the enemy horsemen were repulsed by a body of Hessian infantry.

Observing an additional body of Gendarmes preparing to renew the attack, Cutts requested an immediate reinforcement of cavalry to protect his flank. Five squadrons were promptly ordered to cross the Nebel. Floundering and slithering in the treacherous mud, they made their way with the greatest difficulty through the swamp, to come immediately under the blast of the Gendarmes' musketoons,

After the battle. Tallard (*right*) surrenders to Marlborough.

fired from the saddle. Without a moment's hesitation the British went in with the sword, but they came under a scorching flank fire from Blenheim and were compelled to fall back.

While the British Horse were still struggling to re-form, the first line of the enemy cavalry came hurtling down the slope at the gallop, breaking up the disordered regiments so badly that, had the enemy second line seized this moment to charge, their opponents must have been thrust back into the Nebel.

It was unquestionably a moment of crisis, which Marlborough resolved by ordering up some Danish and Hanoverian squadrons, which had crossed higher up stream, and with these drove the enemy back; the British Horse were given time to reorganize.

Another attempt on Blenheim took the assailants as far as the outskirts of the village; but they could penetrate no further, and were ordered to take up a sheltered position and keep the defenders under fire.

In the meantime the four lines of Marlborough's main

army had slipped and slithered their way down to the Nebel, and crossed the stream, with the infantry drawn up to cover the passage of the Horse. A sharp but relatively brief tussle had driven the Irish Brigade in the French service from Oberglau, and thus the central passage of the stream had finally been assured.

News from Prince Eugene, on the right, was that he was holding his own even if three consecutive attacks had, after a promising start, brought no positive result.

But by this time Marlborough had got all his cavalry across the Nebel and the treacherous terrain bordering the far bank, and had formed them in two strong lines with which to attack the enemy centre.

But with the mounts all heated and blown, the British Horse was still in the process of taking up station when the enemy cavalry bore down full upon them, momentarily pushing them back to the very edge of the stream. The pursuit, however, was swiftly checked by the fire of the supporting infantry, which was so fierce that those left of the enemy cavalry experienced considerable difficulty in making good their retreat.

At last with all his cavalry across the Nebel and re-organized, Marlborough was ready for a mass assault. Nine battalions sent forward by Tallard were mown down by artillery and musketry fire. The French Horse, ordered to go to their support, failed to advance. Marlborough's troopers, riding down the remnants of these shattered battalions, so alarmed Marsin's contingent of Horse that they 'changed position right back', creating a fatal gap between the troops on the left wing and those still holding on in Blenheim.

Realising the catastrophe which threatened him, Tallard ordered Marsin to move to the right and the Blenheim garrison to move troops to the left, to reconstitute resistance in the centre. But the order came too late to be put into effect. Marlborough had marshalled his cavalry for a final attack and personally led them up the slope. 'The French horsemen, instead of riding forward to the encounter, fired feebly from the saddle, and, then turning, fled.' Thirty squadrons made for the Danube, west of Blenheim, pursued

Right: the French cavalry attempted a retreat across the Danube.

by the Prussian cavalry. The great stream lay directly in the fugitives' path, another stream and an impassable swamp was to their flank. A few of the more hardy dashed into the water and sought to make their passage to the distant shore; others crept along the bank and tried to make their way to Hochstadt, where they were to find themselves completely cut off, together with another horde that had fled the field. Hundreds were drowned, hundreds cut down, a vast number taken captive.

Only Marsin, over on the left, contrived to escape in the growing dusk, together with a remnant of his forces.

But Blenheim itself had still to be taken. Too crowded together for effective defence, the French tried desperately to break out, only to be twice herded back. Then, as a mass assault on the village was being organized, the garrison proposed a parley. But Marlborough would consider nothing but unconditional surrender. In shame and resentment the Regiment Navarre burnt its colours rather than yield them. While terms were being argued, Sir James Abercromby of the Royal Regiment of Foot rode up to the ensign of the nearest enemy formation and coolly relieved him of his flag, raising it high above his head to demonstrate that the whole body of the French had capitulated.

Enemy losses had come to 12,000 killed or wounded, and 14,000 made captive, together with all their cannon and stores and some 300 colours. Allied losses totalled 4,500 killed and 7,500 wounded, of which the British dead numbered 670, and their wounded something over 1,500. In due course bounties totalling £64,013 were distributed among the British, of which £4,000 went to the rank and file.

Blenheim by no means saw the end of the War of the Spanish Succession. There was still much hard fighting to be done. But it marked the turning point. For with the overwhelming victory on the banks of the Nebel followed by Rooke's seizure of Gibraltar and his success in the subsequent naval engagement of Malaga, plus the capture of Carthagena, Alicante, Majorca, Sardinia, Minorca and Newfoundland, the initiative had clearly passed into the hands of the Western Alliance, with the ultimate Peace of Utrecht to give Gallic ambitions at least a temporary quietus.

QUEBEC 1759

In 1753 the rivalry between the French and British in the borderlands of their respective North American territories came to a head with the construction by the French of two forts. The first was at Presq'ile, on the south-eastern shore of Lake Erie, and the second, known as Fort le Boeuf, was strategically sited to command the upper waters of the Alleghany and the Ohio.

When the news of this encroachment reached Governor Robert Dinwiddie of Virginia, he at once despatched an emissary to the commandant at Fort le Boeuf demanding his immediate withdrawal from territory 'so notoriously known to be the property of the Crown of England'.

Dinwiddie's choice of representative was Major George Washington of the Virginia Militia. When the French Commandant contemptuously rejected the demand for his withdrawal, it was Washington who was ultimately appointed to command the armed force mobilized to ensure the expulsion of the French from their intrusive outpost.

The outcome was that Washington suffered a humiliating defeat and surrender in an encounter with the intruders at Great Meadows, and was released from captivity only on the

George Washington.

guarantee that the Virginians would 'not attempt to erect any works beyond the mountains for the space of a year'. Hostages for the safe return of certain French prisoners, taken by Washington in an earlier skirmish, included a certain Captain Robert Stobo, whose subsequent detention in Quebec had consequences his captors were to regret.

In Britain, even with an over-extended Royal Navy and a military establishment woefully under strength, the news of Washington's reverse clearly demanded retaliatory measures by the home government. But a combined force of British regulars and provincial levies, under the command of General Edward Braddock, launched in due course against the French and their Indian allies, met with a defeat even more devastating than that suffered earlier by Washington.

So far as the American theatre of operations was concerned, by 1759 an overall plan was devised for a three-prong assault on the French with the object of capturing the metropolitan centres of Quebec and Montreal, together with the intrusive outpost of Fort Duquesne, on the Monongahela – the objective which Braddock had so signally failed to secure in 1755.

As a preliminary to the ascent of the St Lawrence river and the investment of Quebec, it was essential to capture Louisbourg, the French naval base on Cape Breton Island. For this task a force of 14,000 men was put under the command of General Jeffrey Amherst, one of whose brigade commanders was James Wolfe.

Wolfe, though only thirty-two years of age, had already served in seven campaigns. Thin, spindly and singularly unsoldierly in appearance, some said of him that he was 'a meddlesome young fool', while others affirmed that he was 'by far the best hope among the younger commanders'.

Louisbourg was garrisoned by 3,000 of the best troops France could muster, supported by an exceptionally powerful artillery, while its harbour gave anchorage to five Gallic ships of the line and seven frigates. However, seven weeks' hard-pressed siege, supported by a sturdy naval force commanded by 'Wry-necked Dick' – as Admiral Edward Boscawen was invariably termed by sailor and soldier alike – brought Louisbourg's Governor de Drucour seeking honourable terms of capitulation. Louisbourg's submission ended with the surrender of 5,600 prisoners-of-war, over 200

William Pitt.
Left, above: James Wolfe.
A victory medal.

Soldiers at Quebec. *Left*: a French dragoon. *Right*: a British infantryman.

cannon and some 5,000 firelocks.

The way was now clear for the ascent of the St Lawrence and the attempt on the powerfully fortified city of Quebec. But it was not to be Jeffrey Amherst's fate to take command of this particular enterprise. For elsewhere operations had gone anything but well. Under the fumbling leadership of General James Abercromby, the assault on Fort Ticonderoga, the Gallic stronghold protecting Montreal from attack by way of the Hudson river – Lake Champlain route, had proved a costly failure. The only course was to replace Abercromby by Amherst for the central drive, and entrust the attempt on Quebec to his most experienced brigadier – James Wolfe.

Early in June 1759 the convoy, commanded by Admiral Saunders, and transporting some 8,500 troops, cleared

Louisbourg and headed for the mouth of the St Lawrence. The river was notorious for its navigational hazards, but, with careful piloting by the ever-reliable James Cook, by 26 June Wolfe had been landed, unopposed, on the Ile d'Orleans. From this position he surveyed Quebec and the strongly fortified Beauport lines, four miles distant across the intervening basin and stretching eastwards for eight miles along the waterway's northern bank to the river and falls of Montmorenci, affording shelter for the bulk of the 14,000 men of the French garrison. On the southern bank of the St Lawrence, a little downstream from Quebec, Point Lévis was so obviously a position from which fire could be brought to bear on the citadel that Brigadier Robert Monckton was sent to take immediate possession of it.

After several attempts to destroy the British fleet by loosing fireships at their anchorage had been frustrated by the courage and enterprise of Saunders's bluejackets, preparations were speeded up for a combined attack on the Beauport lines. Unfortunately, somewhat inadequate reconnaissance failed to reveal the existence of the 'Beauport Bank', a wide expanse of shallows in front of the enemy position, which rendered it impossible for the fleet to close within effective bombarding range. Furthermore, a ledge

Settlers dispossessed.

running short of the flats so fatally broke up the assault crafts' approach that the attack on the enemy position was anything but well co-ordinated.

Desperately the scattered groups sought to make good their footing, 'but the French troops and Canadians in their lines poured upon them a hailstorm of musket-balls and buckshot, and dead and wounded in numbers rolled together down the slope'. At this critical juncture a hovering summer

Daylight assault on the French positions. 31 July 1759.

storm burst in a positive deluge of rain, and the grassy slopes became so sodden and treacherous that controlled movement upon them was impossible. Realising that the whole venture had gone woefully awry, Wolfe gave the order for withdrawal. With their dead, wounded and missing totalling close on 500, the troops scrambled back into their boats and sullenly withdrew out of range.

There followed a period of stagnation during which Wolfe could think of no more constructive course than to lay waste all the settlements in the vicinity of Quebec, in the hope of provoking desertion among the Canadian militia and exhausting the colony generally.

Quebec's military commander, the Marquis of Montcalm, immediately loosed his Indians and 'white Indians' in a series of counter-raids on the British outposts; and save for these savage forays military activity temporarily ceased.

It was on Admiral Saunders's initiative that HMS *Sutherland* and several smaller vessels passed upstream of Quebec, to be followed in due course by a detachment of troops, which was landed on the south bank in a strong position from which they were admirably placed to harry Montcalm's lines of communication with Montreal – on which Amherst was steadily continuing to advance.

With Wolfe temporarily laid low by sickness, after prolonged discussion between his brigadiers and Admiral Saunders the idea emerged for a forced landing at some point on the north bank of the St Lawrence *above* Quebec, so as to tackle the city's defences from the rear. Visual reconnaissance of the opposite bank from the river's southern shore to pick out a landing-place at the foot of the high, almost vertical and heavily timbered cliffs did not overlook the potentialities of a little cove known as the Ans de Foulon. Any doubts as to the suitability of this particular spot for a landing place were happily set at rest by the information forthcoming from Captain Robert Stobo, recently escaped from his lengthy detention in the city as a prisoner of war, which had in no sense prevented him from becoming intimately acquainted with its environs. Stobo's testimony being fully endorsed by another escaped prisoner of war, Captain Patrick MacKellar, the decision was taken to put the operation in hand without delay.

On 12 September intelligence reached British headquarters that on the next ebb tide a convoy of provisions would seek to steal down river to Quebec. This was precisely the 'cover' necessary to give the British plan of operations a reasonable chance of success.

Thus at 1 a.m. on the following night thirty boats, bearing Wolfe and 1,700 men, set forth to make their landing at the Ans de Foulon, a feint by the vessels still opposite Beauport serving to distract attention from the real point of attack. As Wolfe and the boats full of troops crept quietly downstream, with the sloops and frigates stealing silently in their wake: 'when ye first corps for disembarkation was passing down ye N. Side of ye River', Brigadier Townshend subsequently recorded, 'and ye French Centries on ye banks challeng'd our boats, Captain Frazer, who had been in ye Dutch service & spoke french – answered – "*la france and vive le roi*", on which ye french Centinels ran along ye shore crying "*laissez les passer ils sont nos Gens, avec provisions*".' As had been hoped, the assault force had been mistaken for the convoy bringing supplies for Montcalm.

The British forces scaling the Heights of Abraham.

Once ashore, the Light Infantry swiftly scaled the cliffs and overpowered the Canadian picket allocated to keep watch and ward over the Ans de Foulon; whose commander they found comfortably snugged down in bed!

With the bluejackets lustily engaged in helping to haul a cannon and ammunition to the cliff-top, 'before the sun was well up the whole force of forty-five hundred men had accomplished the ascent, and were filing across the plain at the summit of the heights.'

With cool deliberation, the British leaders had accepted a very considerable risk. In Quebec itself and the adjacent Beauport lines Montcalm commanded a numerically superior body of troops; a mere eight miles upstream his subordinate, Bourgainville, could deploy a body of men sufficiently numerous dangerously to menace the meagre force Wolfe had detached to protect his rear. But as Wolfe had once observed, 'War is an option of risks', and he had deliberately elected to challenge the greatest of them all. So the enemy batteries at nearby Sillery and Samos, which had opened fire at the rearmost of Wolfe's procession of boats, were promptly tackled and as promptly silenced by the men of Colonel William Howe's Light Infantry, and thus this particular threat was eliminated.

Pressing forward to reconnoitre, Wolfe found that the

ground on which he stood formed part of what was known as the Plains of Abraham, a plateau about a mile wide, on the eastern end of which stood Quebec.

It was upon this bleak open plateau that Wolfe drew up his men in single line of battle, with his only gun in their centre. With Bourgainville in his rear, kept precariously in check by Howe and his Light Infantry, it was far from a favourable position; but the troops were in good heart and confident of their ability to get the better of their opponents, as Sergeant Ned Botwood's popular doggerel had made abundantly clear:

Come, each death-dealing dog who dares venture his neck,
Come, follow the hero that goes to Quebec;
And ye that love fighting, shall soon have enough;
Wolfe commands us, my boys; we shall give them hot stuff.

It had been a thoroughly disturbed night in the Beauport lines, for the feint attack organized by Admiral Saunders had proved highly effective. At an hour after midnight 'a great noise of boats was heard', and the troops hurriedly took up station in their entrenchments, remaining uneasily on the alert the whole night through.

The death of James Wolfe. He was 32 years old.

It was not until dawn that a badly scared Canadian arrived with the news that the British had made good their landing at the Ans de Foulon, scaled the heights, and were deploying on the Plains of Abraham. At first the man's story was met with blank disbelief, but as further reports brought confirmation of the claim, orders were sent to Bourgainville to move in on the British rear, while Montcalm in person led out the troops hurried up from the Beauport lines, forming his line of battle some 600 yards from the position taken up by the British. In all, he had succeeded in mustering some 5,000 men.

It is clear, however, that considerable confusion prevailed. The French troops at the extreme end of the Beauport lines either failed to receive the order to join the main body or it reached them too late to be of service; while the officer commanding the artillery in Quebec refused to furnish the field force with more than three of his twenty-five field-guns, declaring that the balance must be retained for the defence of the city walls.

The action opened with the fire of the swarm of Canadian and Indian sharpshooters, for there was admirable cover for

them on the flanks and among the scattered bushes on the British front. Wolfe immediately threw out skirmishers to deal with this growing menace, while the 15th Foot and the Light Infantry were called up to strengthen the flank still further. Thus the rear-guard and wellnigh half the reserve were absorbed in the fight almost from the outset.

Meanwhile Montcalm's three field guns had opened fire, and were replied to with great effect by the single British piece on the Sillery road.

Confusion and uncertainty had so delayed the deployment of the main body of the French that it was not until close on 10 a.m. that Montcalm, mounted on his black charger, led his regular infantry into action, supported on its flanks by yet more Canadian militia.

The English troops, who, until this development, had been lying prone, sprang to their feet and stood at the ready, with their arms at the 'recover'. At a range of 200 yards the French opened a scattered and generally ineffective spatter of shots. Wolfe was hit in the wrist, but made little of his wound, merely wrapping a handkerchief about it as he called to his men to stand steady and reserve their fire. Only the solitary field gun continued to pound the advancing lines with searing grape-shot.

It was not until the ill-aligned enemy front ranks were within forty yards of the British bayonet tips that Wolfe

Marquis de Montcalm. *Right*: his death at Quebec.

ordered his men to fire; and at the word the red-coated array let loose a crashing volley which roared forth from end to end of the line as though fired by a single weapon.

From beyond the billowing cloud of smoke arose the agonized cries of the stricken, the clash of their dropped arms, and a babel of furious oaths. As the smoke cleared, Montcalm was seen to be galloping frantically up and down the shattered ranks, striving to restore them to some sort of order. Then, after another massed discharge from the British line, Wolfe gave the word to advance and complete the rout with bayonet and claymore. The only effective enemy fire was that of a few sharpshooters, sniping from the shelter of the scrub.

It was a missile fired by one of these marksmen that struck Wolfe in the groin, but he barely paused and was again striding forward when another bullet pierced his lungs. Still staggering forward, he called urgently to the nearest officer, 'Support me, support me, lest my gallant fellows should see me fall.'

Minden, 1758. The Seven Years War was fought in Europe as well as overseas – Minden was another French defeat.

Helped to stagger to the rear, his absence was scarcely noticed as the victorious British lines pressed forward. A considerable show of resistance was still maintained by the enemy sharpshooters, but, with Montcalm shot through the body and only just able to stay on his horse, the whole French line crumpled and fled in wild confusion towards the sanctuary offered by the city's walls.

Wolfe was brought to the rear: 'on being asked if he would have a surgeon, he replied, "It is needless, it is all over with me." One of them then cried out, "They run, see how they run." "Who runs?" demanded the prostrate General, like a person aroused from sleep. The officer answered, "The Enemy, Sir; Egad they give way everywhere."' Hastily giving orders for measures that would cut off any hope of the enemy's retreat into the shelter of the Beauport lines, Wolfe, 'turning on his side, added, "Now God be praised, I will die in peace," and thus expired.'

Now that Wolfe was dead and Brigadier Monckton brought down by a musket wound, the command devolved on

Brigadier Townshend. With the failure of an attempt by Bourgainville to attack his rear, he was in strong position to press the investment of Quebec and its demoralized garrison, which capitulated on 17 September.

But the fall of the city by no means brought an end to the fighting. In the April of 1760 Brigadier Murray – left in command in Quebec – was very roughly handled in St Foy, a little below Cap Rouge. But the reappearance of the British fleet added appreciably to Murray's strength, while Amherst was moving steadily if slowly on Montreal.

The capital's submission in the September of 1760 was followed by the capitulation of the western posts of Detroit, Miamis and Machillimackinac, and with that Canada passed unreservedly into British possession.

In general, the acquisition was enthusiastically acclaimed. But as the late eighteenth-century diarist, John Knyveton, perceptively observed: 'Perhaps it is a pity we conquered Canada; had the French remained upon their border, the Americans, for safety's sake, would have remained close-knit to the country from which they sprang.'

It was a comment whose prescience the events of 1775–83 were only too abundantly to endorse.

Europe's boundaries, 1756–63.

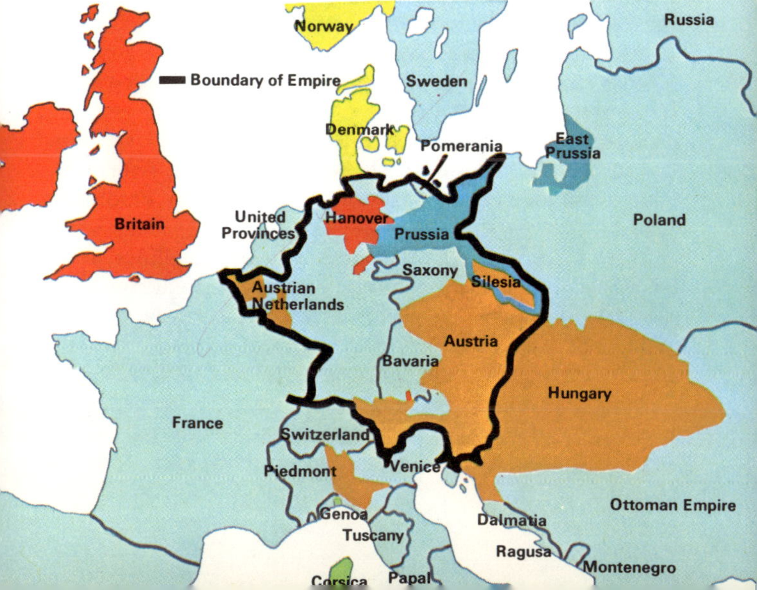

The destruction of the statue of George III by New Yorkers, 1776.

SARATOGA 1777

On that fatal day of April 1775, when the confrontation between the British troops out of Boston and the Minute Men and militia on Lexington Common culminated in 'the shot heard round the world', the war of words between the American colonists and their British kindred finally erupted into a clash of arms.

With the British troops in Boston under close-pressed siege and George Washington appointed to the supreme command of the patriot militia, Benedict Arnold set about the successive capture of all the posts on Lake George and Lake Champlain, the most direct route for a descent on Canada.

True to precedent, the outbreak of hostilities found Britain with an army entirely inadequate numerically for the task to which it was committed. Measures were put in hand not only to increase its strength to 40,000, but also to amplify its numbers by hiring the services of a number of German mercenaries of extremely variable quality. Little was done, however, to restore an equally neglected navy.

With the garrison in Boston reduced by some forty per

cent as the result of the Bunker Hill battle, the seaport was evacuated, the troops being transferred to Nova Scotia to await reinforcement.

While General Howe marked time in Halifax, General Guy Carleton, the British Governor in Canada, had repulsed Arnold from before Quebec, driven him up-river, reclaimed Montreal, and pressed his pursuit along the shores of Lake Champlain to within sight of the stronghold of Ticonderoga.

By the August of 1776 Howe had been sufficiently reinforced to sail into the waters approaching New York, land his troops to win the battle of Long Island, occupy New York, and, after the defeat of Washington at White Plains and the occupation of the two rebel forts on the Hudson waterway, to force his adversary to seek refuge beyond the Delaware river. Washington's riposte, in the form of his Christmastide raid on Trenton, was of greater propaganda value than of fundamental military significance.

Thus the imminence of the campaigning season of 1777

A recruiting bill for Washington's army.

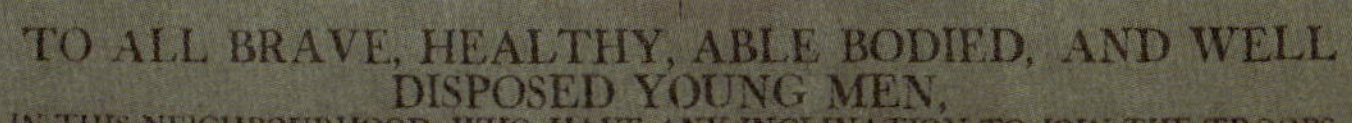

TO ALL BRAVE, HEALTHY, ABLE BODIED, AND WELL DISPOSED YOUNG MEN,
IN THIS NEIGHBOURHOOD, WHO HAVE ANY INCLINATION TO JOIN THE TROOPS, NOW RAISING UNDER
GENERAL WASHINGTON,
FOR THE DEFENCE OF THE
LIBERTIES AND INDEPENDENCE
OF THE UNITED STATES,
Against the hostile designs of foreign enemies,

TAKE NOTICE,

THAT *Tuesday, Wednesday, Thursday, Friday and Saturday at Spotswood in Middlesex* county, attendance will be given by *Lieutenant Reading* with his music and recruiting party of company in *Major Shute's Battalion* of the 11th regiment of infantry, commanded by Lieutenant Colonel Aaron Ogden, for the purpose of receiving the enrollment of such youth of SPIRIT, as may be willing to enter into this HONOURABLE service.

The ENCOURAGEMENT at this time, to enlist, is truly liberal and generous, namely, a bounty of TWELVE dollars, an annual and fully sufficient supply of good and handsome cloathing, a daily allowance of a large and ample ration of provisions, together with SIXTY dollars a year in GOLD and SILVER money on account of pay, the whole of which the soldier may lay up for himself and friends, as all articles proper for his subsistance and comfort are provided by law, without any expence to him.

Those who may favour this recruiting party with their attendance as above, will have an opportunity of hearing and seeing in a more particular manner, the great advantages which these brave men will have, who shall embrace this opportunity of spending a few happy years in viewing the different parts of this beautiful continent, in the honourable and truly respectable character of a soldier, after which, he may, if he pleases return home to his friends, with his pockets FULL of money and his head COVERED with laurels.

GOD SAVE THE UNITED STATES.

found both sides poised in a posture whose exploitation offered a number of alternatives.

It was at this juncture that General John Burgoyne put forward a plan for an advance from Canada by way of Crown Point to Albany and the Hudson river, the alternative routes being either down Lake George, or by South Bay and overland to Skenesborough. Concurrently, a diversion by a small body of troops from Oswego should be made along the Mohawk river, to its confluence with the Hudson. Co-operation by a force based on New York would secure the line of the Hudson, thus inhibiting support from New England for the rebellious southern provinces, and vice versa.

Unfortunately, at this crucial hour the Secretary of State for the Colonies – responsible for the direction of all operations for their retention – was Lord George Germain. Court-martialled and dismissed from the Army for his pusillanimity when in command of the cavalry at the battle of Minden, he had nonetheless contrived to bribe and inveigle his way into politics to the extent of being able to secure appointment to the one office in which a native genius for bungling and ill-timed interference could cause the most mischief.

Burgoyne arrived back in Canada on 6 May, and immediately set about implementing the plan which had won the government's approval, confident that directions would

Burgoyne. After Reynolds. *Right*: Washington crossing the Delaware.

be sent to Howe to conform to the overall strategy. In point of fact, however, even if Howe's copies of the General Orders were ever drawn up and signed – which is extremely doubtful – it is certain that he never received them. Thus at the very time when he should have been concluding arrangements to ensure junction with the force striking for Albany and the Hudson, he had embarked his troops and set sail for the Chesapeake, leaving no more than a minimal garrison, under General Henry Clinton, to protect New York.

In complete ignorance of this fatal divergence from the agreed strategy, early in June Burgoyne marshalled his troops prior to their embarkation on Lake Champlain, the first move in the 'dash' to Albany and the Hudson. In all, his forces totalled some 7,000 officers and men, of whom nearly half were German. They were amplified by a few score Canadian *coureurs de bois* and Indians, and accompanied by close on 1,000 camp followers.

Burgoyne's first objective was Fort Ticonderoga, at the junction of Lake Champlain with Lake George. The stronghold, manned by a garrison of 3,000, was obviously in a

position to offer an obstinate defence. But, as the enterprising artillery officer, 'Philippe of Minden', was quick to note, an eminence called Sugar Hill dominated the whole defensive complex. If only artillery could be posted on its slopes, Ticonderoga would lie at the assailants' mercy. The fact that the ascent of the mount was in some places almost precipitous was robustly disregarded, Philippe hardily declaring that 'where a goat can go a man can go, and where a man can go he can drag a gun.' Having, with tremendous physical exertion, installed a battery on Sugar Hill's summit, its guns so obviously dominated the American position that General St Clair, realising the hopelessness of his situation, abandoned the post, retreating by way of Castleton, to Skenesborough with the British doggedly plodding along the same route in pursuit.

Movement southwards from Skenesborough to Fort Edward was particularly difficult and arduous. The way led across country full of swamps and creeks, necessitating the construction of no less than forty bridges, one of which was two miles long. Moreover, the American leader, Philip Schuyler, had instructed his followers to fell trees across the twenty-mile line of march, so that they lay 'every which way', reducing the rate of progress to a mile a day. Thus time was afforded for the patriots, working on interior lines, to mobilize more and more forces with which to oppose Burgoyne when a suitable opportunity occurred.

From Fort Edward the next objective was Battenkill, five miles from Saratoga. At this juncture news from the subsidiary force moving on the Mohawk was far from satisfactory; while with the main body – depleted by the troops left to garrison Ticonderoga – there was constant trouble with such Indians as still accompanied the expedition. In addition, a growing shortage of draught-horses put the movement of the artillery train in increasing jeopardy. Finally, the retarded rate of progress had so worn away the reserve of stores that the troops were threatened with a disastrous lack of provisions. The only remedy available was for the British commander to supplement his supplies at American expense. Learning that the New England militia had established a magazine at Bennington, some thirty miles south-east of Fort Edward, 'Gentleman Johnny' Burgoyne detailed Colonel Baum and a force of German troops, Canadian volunteers and a number of professing loyalists to raid the depot. At the same time Burgoyne's main force moved down the east bank of the Hudson, an advance party crossing the river to Saratoga, while a detachment remained at Battenkill, five miles from Saratoga, on the direct road from Bennington.

Washington at the Battle of Princeton.

thirty days, he pushed on to Saratoga.

Almost immediately, however, he found his way barred by a strong and steadily increasing force deployed in a position carefully selected and strongly fortified by the Polish military engineer Tadeusz Kosciusco. It was commanded by the erstwhile British officer Horatio ('Granny') Gates, whose appointment over Philip Schuyler owed less to his superior military skill than to a highly cultivated faculty for backstairs political intrigue. He could, however, call on the services of the far more able Benedict Arnold, while, as Burgoyne himself ruefully noted, 'wherever the King's forces point, militia to the number of three or four thousand assemble in a few hours', many of them under the command of such veteran leaders as John Stark and Daniel Morgan.

With the Americans deployed in their position on Bemis Heights, Burgoyne quickly noted that there was a hill on the enemy left which commanded the whole of their position, but which was still unoccupied. If this eminence could be seized and artillery hauled into position, the enemy line of

'Enheartened by assurances of the ready help he would receive from local loyalists, Baum pushed on until he ran into a strong force of the local militia – led by fiery John Stark – who were speedily amplified by the very individuals who had earlier been posing as loyalists.' Outnumbered and virtually surrounded, Baum fought back with dogged courage, seeking desperately to gain contact with the supports sent out under Colonel Breymann.

When the survivors of this expensive and entirely unproductive mission contrived to struggle back to the main body, Burgoyne found himself the poorer by 500 men and four field pieces. In effect, normal wastage plus the Bennington losses had reduced 'Gentleman Johnny's' force to some 5,700 officers and men. But every encouragement had been given him to look for substantial support from Howe or from Clinton in New York; so having with considerable difficulty gathered in supplies for approximately

Right: Green Mountain Boys, a Vermont local force.

battle could be raked from end to end. It was to further this design that 'Gentleman Johnny' drew up his general plan of action. His force was to advance in three columns. That on the left under, General Riedesel, supported by Phillips and his artillery, was to follow the river road and pin down the American right. The British right column, under Brigadier Simon Frazer, was to make a wide detour to gain possession of the hill which enfiladed the enemy entrenchments. The attack in the centre was to be led by Burgoyne himself. As the whole area was thick with trees, the intimation that Burgoyne and Frazer had joined hands and that Riedesel was to go into action was to be the discharge of three signal guns.

The action opened with the expulsion of an American picket from an outlying dwelling, known as Freman's Farm, immediately in Burgoyne's front. Then, with Frazer in possession of the hill on the right and the three guns booming out the signal for a general advance, there was, as one survivor wrote, 'such an explosion of fire, I never had any idea of before, and the heavy artillery joining in concert like great peals of thunder, assisted by the echoes of the woods, almost deafened us with the noise.'

Locked in deadly conflict in the centre, at this stage the revitalized enemy initiative owed everything to Benedict Arnold. Seeking to turn his opponents' right, he was extremely roughly handled by Simon Frazer. Undismayed, he swung to launch a fierce attack on 'Gentleman Johnny's' centre, and there followed a tussle in which, as Lamb subsequently noted, 'Men, particularly Officers, dropped every moment on each side. Several of the Americans placed themselves in high trees and as often as they could distinguish an Officer's uniform, they took him off by deliberately aiming at his person.' As at Bunker Hill, the British officers, conspicuous in their gold-laced uniforms and glittering gorgets, were the particular targets of the men of Daniel Morgan's ranger corps – backwoods-marksmen armed with that Kentucky or Frontier rifle which unquestionably qualified as a first-class weapon of precision.

With Burgoyne and his opponents locked in combat in the centre, it was the appearance of Riedesel on the

Above: British officer. *Below*: Royal Artilleryman. *Right*: the battles prior to Saratoga.

Americans' right flank and the arrival on the field of additional artillery which determined the immediate issue of the conflict. Darkness approaching, the Americans fell back on their prepared positions and Burgoyne and his men bivouacked on the ground they had won. But there was no escaping the fact the 'Gentleman Johnny's' losses were over 500 officers and man – a casualty rate he was certainly in no position to afford.

But news had contrived to get through that Clinton and a body of troops from New York were successfully fighting

Burgoyne surrenders.

their way up the Hudson; and it was the hope that a conjunction of the two forces would compel the Americans into retreat, leaving the river line under British control, which fortified Burgoyne's determination to renew his offensive against Gates. And this despite the fact that intelligence had reached him that the subsidiary expedition on the Mohawk had met with outright failure, and that a body of enemy troops had captured the British flotilla on Lake George and now lay across his communications with Canada.

Near midday on 7 October Burgoyne again set his troops in motion. With the Germans in the centre and the British on the flanks, he formed his tenuous line three-quarters of a mile from the American left, such few Indians and Canadian auxiliaries as still remained with him stealing off to try and take the enemy in the rear. But before the British and their German comrades got fairly under way they were halted by a furious attack by Morgan against Burgoyne's left flank. Arnold had also thrown himself into the thick of the fight, his example spurring his followers to a fury of attack which became increasingly difficult to withstand.

Wheeling back at right angles to cover the left flank, the British Grenadiers met the onset with such firmness that the Americans hastened to bring up some 4,000 additional troops with which to extend their assault to the Germans of Burgoyne's left-centre. One battalion of Brunswickers almost immediately gave way. Virtually at the same moment, a separate column of overwhelming strength appeared on the scene to turn Burgoyne's right flank, a movement only partially arrested by Frazer hastily switching over the Light Infantry and 24th Foot to cover the retreat. Meanwhile the Grenadiers on the left gave way before overwhelming numbers, and once again Frazer was obliged to transfer his dwindling detachment for their support. It was while this movement was being carried into effect that Simon Frazer fell, mortally wounded by the bullet from a sniper perched on the limb of a tree.

It was plain that only withdrawal to his fortified lines could hope to save what few were left of 'Gentleman Johnny's' battered forces, and he sent an order for the artillery to retire while some protection could still be afforded it by the infantry. But the aide-de-camp entrusted with handing over the order was mortally wounded before he could deliver it, and thus further valuable time was lost in which the Americans could re-marshal their forces.

With Phillips and Riedesel covering the movement, Burgoyne ultimately succeeded in withdrawing his hard-pressed troops in reasonably good order to the shelter of their entrenchments, although not without the sacrifice of six guns, whose teams had been shot down to the last horse and man.

Ignoring the lethargic Gates, Arnold immediately launched an attack on his opponents before they had been given time to settle themselves in their new positions. The first assault, delivered against Burgoyne's right centre, was beaten back. However, the extreme right flank, being defended only by Canadian irregulars, was easily pierced, although the Germans, hurrying to the scene, fought until nightfall.

With a crumpled right flank, Burgoyne withdrew his army in perfectly good order to some heights immediately above the river but was ultimately forced to withdraw to Saratoga, abandoning 500 sick and wounded to the enemy.

Benedict Arnold unhorsed.

Daylight on the morning of 9 October revealed the Americans entrenching the heights on the opposite side of the river to bar the British from crossing. Retreat to Fort Edward was ruled out by the fact that a strong force of the enemy was entrenched across the line of withdrawal. With Gates in command of between 18,000 and 20,000 men, Burgoyne and his battered remnant were surrounded, desperately short of supplies and with no news of Clinton to give them some faint hope that succour was at hand.

Yet for a few days Burgoyne hung on, and it was not until the morning of the 14th, with his troops almost starving, that he made overtures for a capitulation, the terms of which were finally concluded on the 17th.

It was agreed that the 3,500 British and German troops still 'fit for duty' should march out with the honours of war, pile their arms and be conducted forthwith to Boston for shipment to England, on the understanding that they would serve no more in America. It was an honourable agreement, and the formalities of surrender were conducted with the chivalrous courtesy and consideration that is never denied by brave men to vanquished but equally courageous opponents. It was the American Congress which shamefully reneged on the agreement to return the prisoners to England, despite the remonstrances of Washington and his senior officers, who were as indignant at this outrageous betrayal of a formal agreement as the British people themselves.

Saratoga, of course, gave an enormous boost to the patriots' enthusiasm and confidence, with a corresponding lowering of morale to those who still dared to harbour loyalist sentiments. Even more significantly, it encouraged first France, then Spain and then Holland to declare war against the British Crown, while the smouldering enmity of Russia, Denmark and Sweden – the main sources of Britain's naval supplies – found expression in the formation of the first Armed Neutrality compact.

As Lord Stanhope so cogently expressed it: "Even of those great conflicts, in which hundreds of thousands have been engaged, and the tens of thousands have fallen, none has been more fruitful of results than this surrender of thirty-five hundred fighting men at Saratoga.'

WATERLOO

Having with 'a whiff of grapeshot', ruthlessly suppressed a domestic uprising on the part of the Sections (Wards) of Paris in the insurrection of the 13th Vendemaire, the Republic's new protégé, Napoleon Bonaparte, was in 1796 entrusted with the command of the army of Italy where Austria was fully mobilized and ready to repel any Gallic attempt at conquest in her sphere of influence.

In the outcome, however, with the Austrians defeated all along the line, Italy was plundered with a ruthlessness which in three months bled the country of £53,000,000 in coin and three times that amount in requisitioned goods, not counting innumerable art treasures transferred to Paris.

Thus the pattern was set for a quarter of a century's ruthless combat and spoliation, for as Napoleon climbed from the post of first consul to that of self-elected emperor, it became only too starkly apparent that he was the personification of the age-old intention of the French to keep Europe weak and divided the better to ensure its plunder.

However, two fundamental blunders, the result of over-weening self-confidence, presaged the Corsican's undoing

and the eventual abasement of the country which had so blindly supported him: the swashbuckling sally into Portugal and Spain, which led to the 'running ulcer' of the Peninsular War; and the foolishly inconsequent invasion of Russia in 1812. For as the perceptive military strategist, Baron Henri Jomini, drily commented: 'the Russian Army is a wall which, however far it may retreat, you will always find in front of you.' And so it proved.

It was Napoleon himself who once observed that, 'It does not suffice to gain a victory; you must learn to turn it to advantage.' Yet where the sterile victory of Borodino had been concerned, this was what he had signally failed to do. With his obsession regarding the seizure of capital cities, the lure of an advance on Moscow had been impossible to resist, however ill-provisioned and poorly-equipped his forces might be to embark upon so hazardous an undertaking.

The outcome had been unqualified catastrophe. Of the half million men Napoleon had led into Russia, no more than a few thousand survivors could be counted upon for further service with the *Tricoleur*, while the heavily depleted forces in Spain were further reduced by the need to bolster up the army desperately seeking to hold its own in Germany.

The attack on the Bastille, 1789.

But the 'Sepoy General' – Arthur Wellesley, the future Duke of Wellington, who in India had mastered the art of generalship the hard way – was across the Pyrenees, and Toulouse was in British hands. From the north-east the Allies were steadily converging upon Paris, whose fickle population was already bellowing '*Vive l'Empereur Alexandre*! *Vive le Roi de Prusse*!' So with his own marshals sternly informing him that if he proposed a further resort to arms, they would not support him, on 4 April, 1814, Napoleon signed at Fontainebleau the deed of abdication which restored the throne to the House of Bourbon and committed him to exile on the lonely isle of Elba.

With relief, a war-worn Europe settled down to try to restore its ravished lands, reconstitute its normal flow of commerce, and generally resume a way of life no longer menaced by the thunder of the guns or the tramp of armies.

For Britain the task was seriously retarded by the fact that her armed forces were still committed to the entirely

Valmy, 1792. The Argonne gorge.

irrelevant and unnecessary conflict with the United States.

So far as Europe was concerned, with the Treaty of Paris duly in operation, other weighty matters were referred to the adjudication of the Congress in session in Vienna. So with ill-advised haste the British parliament proceeded to dismantle a large proportion of the country's armed forces, so that by the close of 1814 no less than 47,000 men had been struck off the muster rolls, while in the Royal Navy far too many serviceable vessels had rashly been 'laid up in ordinary'.

Then, like a clap of thunder, came the news that 'Corporal Violette' had escaped from Elba, landed at Fréjus, and was heading for Paris, calling upon his scattered legions to rally to him to free 'la belle France' from the feeble reign of Louis XVIII and the insolent presence of his alien supporters.

But those selfsame supporters were already rallying to the Bourbon's aid, although Louis himself had promptly fled Paris and sought sanctuary in Ghent.

Since the Allies encompassed France in a crescent extending from the Alps to the North Sea, the salient question

Napoleon had to decide was where best to strike at them. Patently the wisest course would be to set about the re-conquest of the Belgian provinces: a victory bulletin dated from Brussels might well persuade the frustrated Allies to resort to diplomacy rather than to rely upon a further appeal to arms.

Having mobilized close on half a million troops, some of whom were detached to guard the Jura, the Alps, the Var

Bonaparte returns from Elba, 1 March 1815.

and the Pyrenees, it was with an army of somewhat varying quality, but totalling 124,000, with 370 guns, that in the second week of June Napoleon set out along the road which led by way of Charleroi and Quatre Bras to Brussels.

With the Corsican's startling reappearance the Allies had immediately made arrangements to put 735,000 men in the field, the British, with the best of their troops in North America, compensating for the fact that even including the Hanoverians and the King's German Legion they could not mobilize more than 37,000, by supporting their coadjutors with substantial subsidies.

It was Napoleon's aim to isolate and defeat in detail either the British or the Prussian army – to which, on their own, he was superior in numbers – before they could concentrate and combine their respective forces; for there was no immediate reason for concern about the Russian and Austrian armies, which were still a considerable distance from France's eastern frontier.

Napoleon's principal handicap was the lack of reliable subordinate commanders: Masséna was too old and worn; Davout was tied to the War Ministry; Bernadotte, as Crown Prince of Sweden, was actually in arms against him; and Soult was a very indifferent substitute as chief of staff for the ever-resourceful Berthier, who had fallen out of a window at Bamberg and broken his neck. But Napoleon had infinite faith in himself and in his ability to carry the day.

With his headquarters in Brussels, Wellington's forces held the line from Ath to Braine-le-Comte, with an outpost at Mons. Blücher, with an army of 117,000, with 296 guns was in position between Dinant and Namur, with an outpost at Charleroi.

Moving with his accustomed speed, Napoleon launched his main attack against Blücher at Ligny, while a detached corps under Marshal Ney was given the task of driving back Wellington's advance guard at Quatre Bras, the cross-roads on the Brussels-Charleroi route where the junction of the Allied forces was designed to ensure mutual support.

In the event, although in command of numerically superior forces, Blücher was very roughly handled at Ligny, the *Feldmarschal* himself being unhorsed and ridden over, while

his troops were driven back in considerable disorder, pursued by a corps under Marshal Grouchy. At Quartre Bras, on the other hand, although suffering substantial losses, the British and their Dutch-Belgian allies were able to hold their ground, eventually drawing off behind a cavalry rearguard to the battle position selected by Wellington at Mount St Jean, south of the Forest of Soignies and barring the route to Brussels.

Disposed along a low plateau which lay across the Brussels road, Wellington's command totalled 67,000 – of which the British element came to 23,000 – with 160 guns. But since the cream of the war-experienced 'Peninsular' regiment were 3,000 miles away across the Atlantic, and the Dutch-Belgian contingent was of doubtful value, the Duke had some excuse for gruffly describing his force as 'an infamous army, very weak and ill-equipped, and with a very inexperienced staff'. There was every reason, therefore, to stand on the defensive until the assistance promised by Blücher – whose troops had been halted and reorganized – could arrive and render the combined armament strong enough to go over to the attack.

A sunken road ran most of the way along Wellington's front, which was bounded on the right by the Chateau Hougoumont with its grounds and orchards, and on the left by the farmhouse of La Haye Sainte and the village of Papellotte, both flanks being strongly held.

After a night of soaking rainfall time had to be given for the ground to dry sufficiently to permit the movement of cavalry and gun-teams. So it was not until 11.30 a.m. that Napoleon, having inspected his cheering troops in their battle stations on the opposite plateau of La Belle Alliance, gave the order for his artillery to open fire. A general cannonade was followed by an intensive blast from eighty guns in the centre, firing grape, canister, round-shot and bags of horse-shoe nails.

This was the preliminary to a forward thrust by four enemy divisions, moving *en echelon* against Wellington's

Wellington and Blücher after Waterloo.

left-centre, and, although the hostile advance suffered heavy casualties, a Dutch-Belgian brigade to all intents and purposes fled in panic. With this, a number of men from a fifth enemy division took possession of the grounds of La Haye Sainte, Dubois's Cuirassiers having ridden down a contingent of Hanoverians sent to the farmhouse garrison's support.

It was at this juncture that the French, seeking to deploy, were struck by a crashing volley and saw the British 5th Division advancing at the charge. At their head their commander, 'rough old, tough old' Thomas Picton, in his battered top hat and nursing beneath his rumpled greatcoat the wound he had sustained two days earlier, was one of the first victims of the enemy counter-fire.

As the men of the 5th and their thinned-out supports continued to press forward, Lord Uxbridge gave the word which set two squadrons of the 1st Life Guards and two of the King's Dragoon Guards hurtling down the slope to 'collide with the French Cuirassiers', as one eye-witness recorded, 'like two walls'. Almost at the same moment the 2nd Life Guards and a squadron of the King's Dragoon Guards struck at Dubois's right flank as his troopers spilled out in some confusion on to the Genappe-Charleroi road. Foremost in the fray was the erstwhile prizefighter, Life Guardsman Shaw, who slew two Cuirassiers in close combat before being struck from the saddle; while Sergeant Ewart captured and bore off the eagle of the French 45th Foot.

From the outset Hougoumont had been the object of sustained attack, the courtyard being cleared of the enemy and the main gate closed only after the most violent hand-to-hand struggle.

At 4 p.m. the third phase of the battle opened with a concentrated bombardment of the Allies' right; the preliminary to a mass attack by the enemy cavalry. To meet it the British battalions formed squares, the gunners firing grape and round-shot up to the very last moment, and then, after rendering their pieces immobile by detaching the near wheel, seeking temporary refuge within the squares – having carefully trundled the disconnected wheels ahead of them.

The squares, moreover, had been drawn up chequerwise,

Above: a French hussar. *Right*: a Prussian infantryman.

so that it was impossible for the enemy cavalry to attack any one of them without coming under the flanking fire of the others. As at Quatre Bras, therefore, the assailants were reduced to an aimless teetering about between the squares, and thus suffered very heavy loss without inflicting compensatory damage. Then with a well-timed counter-attack by the Allied horse, the enemy Cuirassiers were swept clean out of action, while the gunners promptly darted from the shelter of the squares to replace their cannon wheels and bring their pieces once more into action. And in the woodlands beyond Planchenoit Napoleon's 'perspective glass' could pick out the vanguard of Blücher's Prussians, steadily advancing. For, faithful to his promise, the *Feldmarschal,* having contrived to elude the enemy detachment sent to ward him off, was in the process of fulfilling his commitment to come to Wellington's support.

Clearly, it was vital for Napoleon to shatter the stubborn British resistance before the Prussians bore down to assail

The disposition of forces at Waterloo.

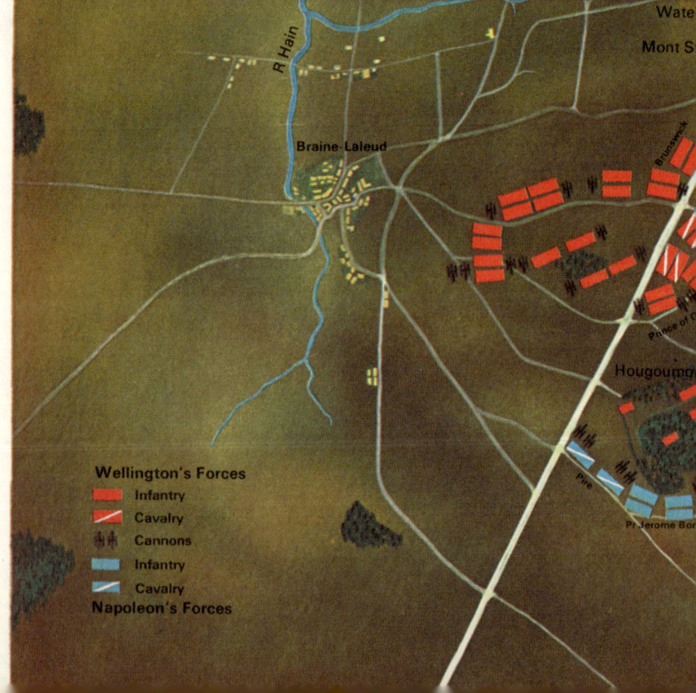

his vulnerable right flank. The defenders of La Haye Sainte had been perilously whittled away; Hougoumont had been penetrated and the Allies' grip on this vital *point d'appui* appreciably loosened. Clearly the moment had arrived to launch a major attempt to shatter the Allied centre.

As an opening move two battalions of the Old Guard were sent to sweep the Prussians out of Planchenoit. Hougoumont ablaze, Napoleon threw in his last reserve – 3,500 of the Imperial Guard. With the intrepid Marshal Ney at their head, in two dense columns they deployed across the low ground between the two plateaus. Above them on the crest were Maitland's British Guards, lying prone to lessen the effect of the enemy artillery, their line prolonged on the right by Colborne's Light Infantry. Steadily, in well-ordered array, strode the men in the towering bearskins, their eagles catching the last fitful gleams of the declining sun, their voices uplifted in the cry of '*Vive l'Empereur*!' To their flanks and rear the whole French line advanced to the veterans' support. Cannon, planted in the intervals of the supporting columns, tore great gaps in the Allies' ranks,

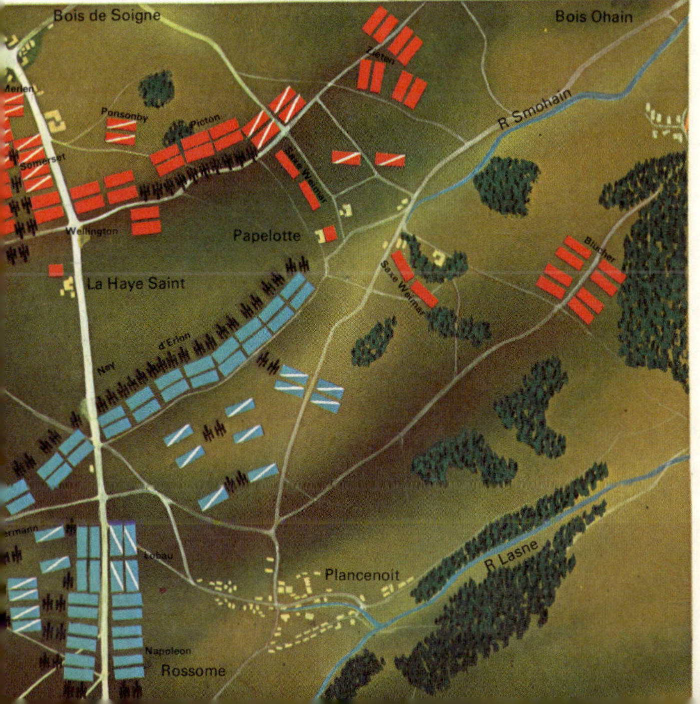

while *voltiguers* and *chasseurs à pied* skirmished ahead up to the defenders' musket muzzles.

With the combat about La Haye Sainte also mounting in renewed intensity, the deep but narrow masses of the Imperial Guard strode steadily up the slope, bearing directly for the point on the ridge where the British Guards were waiting to receive them, while the Allied artillery concentrated their fire on the close-packed ranks.

Ney's horse was shot from under him but, scrambling to his feet, 'the bravest of the brave', conspicuous in his glittering uniform, continued to lead his men on foot.

As the Imperialists approached the plateau's rim, it was Wellington himself who gave the order, 'Up Guards, and make ready!' Maitland's men, crouching hitherto in four-deep formation, sprang to their feet and, at fifty yards, poured a hail of shot into the advancing foe which tumbled

The battle at its height.

their ranks into a welter of death, agony and confusion.

With perfect timing, Sir John Colborne brought up the 52nd to loose a hail of musketry *en enfilade* into the left wing of the Imperial Guardsmen, who swung to return the fire of these new opponents while still striving to maintain their front against Maitland and his 'redcoats'.

But with the unceasing blast of double-shotted guns and small-arm fire tearing their battered ranks to shreds, the Imperialists faltered and began to give ground. Down came the bayonets of the Guards and the 52nd as the Duke's loud call, 'Now Maitland, now's your chance!' sent the two formations surging forward in a charge which swept the Imperialists into stumbling flight. Then, with a forward swing of his hat, Wellington gave the command: 'The whole line will advance!'

It was the end. With the Prussians crowding into action from the direction of Planchenoit and the British sweeping forward across the enemy's collapsing battle-stations,

Napoleon turned his horse's head and rode from the field.

'*Quelle affaire*!' gasped Blücher as he rode up exuberantly to embrace a British colleague who still remained singularly calm and undisturbed.

In Paris, which he reached on 21 June, Napoleon was confronted with the choice of complying with the obvious desire of the Chamber for his abdication, or resorting to mob support to engineer a *coup d'etat* which would inevitably culminate in civil war. In any case the Allies were closing in on him; the Empire was bankrupt; only his own insatiable thirst for conquest stood between France and the peace for which the majority of her people yearned.

Thus on 15 July, 1815, Napoleon surrendered to Captain Maitland aboard the *Bellerophon*, and exile to St Helena ensured that the peace of Europe should stand no risk of further disruption by the man whose megalomania had only too faithfully epitomized that of the people who had encouraged him on his disastrous course.

GETTYSBURG

The gold-rush to California of 1849 and the subsequent discovery of the precious metal in Colorado, while enriching the United States by several hundred million dollars, also gave rise to a problem which was destined to shake the polity of the country to its foundations.

For from the very outset the southern states counted upon acquiring predominant influence in the west, since both were bound together by the arms of the great Mississippi waterway, whose outlet to the sea was also in the south.

But the gold of California and Colorado provided the capital with which the northern entrepreneurs could build the railways which came so swiftly to seam the west, furnishing the means by which the produce of these newly-developed territories could be transported to the profitable markets of the east.

Moreover, the rallying cry of the abolitionists of the western Free-soil Party was 'free soil for a free people', a slogan unlikely to commend itself to those southern states where slavery still played a leading part in the economic

Left: Blücher. *Below*: Ney.
Bottom: Wellington.

structure of the indigenous population.

By 1858 elections for the senate found Abraham Lincoln – running as candidate for Illinois – solemnly pronouncing: 'A house divided against itself cannot stand. I believe this government cannot endure half slave and half free. I do not expect the house to fall, but I expect it will cease to be divided. It will become all one thing or all the other.'

The looming crisis was precipitated when a certain John Brown, a fervent abolitionist, headed a small party of fanatics and free negroes to seize the Federal arsenal at Harper's Ferry. Reports immediately flashed over the wires that the slaves throughout Virginia were rising against their masters, while in the south the terrible prospect of an insurrection of slaves created little less than panic. It called for little imagination to picture the likely devastation of homes and property, the bestialities to which the women and children might be subjected, the virtual disruption of the whole of the southerners' accustomed way of life.

At Harper's Ferry John Brown and his handful of followers were put under siege by an armed force commanded by Colonel Robert E. Lee. After several casualties had been

Abraham Lincoln. From a bronze bust.

suffered on both sides, Brown's final refuge in the armoury engine-house was forced and he and his five remaining followers were taken captive.

Arraigned on a charge of treason, conspiring to foment rebellion, and of murder in the first degree, Brown was sentenced to be hanged. But the tumult he had unleashed increased rather than subsided with his execution.

With Abraham Lincoln's election to follow James Buchanan as President of the United States, and his pronouncement that, once in office, he 'looked forward to seeing slavery put where the people would be satisfied that it was in course of ultimate extinction', there could be no doubt in southern minds that nothing short of secession could preserve this institution so firmly woven into the fabric of their accustomed way of life.

In framing the Declaration of Independence in 1776, its sponsors had been careful to pronounce that 'these united colonies are, and of right ought to be, free and independent States', the word *nation* being carefully eschewed. Equally, the subsequent Federal Constitution in no sense instituted a sovereign body, and it was upon this all-important point that South Carolina's legislative chamber declared the dissolution of the union 'subsisting between South Carolina and the other States under the name of the United States of America'. Within a month Georgia, Alabama, Mississippi and Florida passed similar resolutions; Louisiana seceding a little later, to be followed by Virginia, North Carolina, Tennessee and Arkansas.

Then, in the February of 1861, the representatives of the 'cotton States' met at Montgomery, Alabama, to institute their own indigenous government. A provisional constitution was devised, the name of Confederate States adopted, Jefferson Davis of Mississippi nominated as President and Richmond, Virginia, made capital of the southern states. All subsequent attempts at compromise between north and south were virtually ruled out with the secessionists' seizure of such government property – custom houses, forts, arsenals and navy yards – as lay within their borders, with the exception of Fort Pickens, Key West, the Dry Tortugas and Fort Sumpter in Charleston harbour.

But Lincoln had explicitly pronounced, 'No State upon its own mere motion can lawfully get out of the Union', and any ordinance which sought to bring this about, he averred, was null and void. To such an expression of intent there could only be one outcome – civil war.

The first fatal shots were fired when General Beauregard was directed by the Confederate authorities to demand the surrender of Fort Sumpter in Charleston Harbour and to enforce its capitulation should voluntary submission be refused.

From then on the whole controversy over state rights as opposed to Federal union was submitted to the grim arbitration of the sword.

But President Lincoln's task of subduing an armed rebellion demanded a considerably larger force than the 16,367 officers and men immediately available. For the Confederacy had already enrolled 100,000 volunteers and a large proportion of the officers on the regular establishment, being southerners by birth and political sympathy, had already gone over to the Confederate camp. It was true that 75,000 northern militia could be mobilized by decree but few of them had undergone any real military training. In

Left: General Grant. *Right*: Stonewall Jackson. Opposite: Robert E. Lee.

the outcome, by the end of 1861 the Federal authorities had mobilized 560 infantry regiments, 82 cavalry formations – most of them lacking mounts – and 9 regiments of artillery, some enlisted for three years, some on the wasteful plan of a 'nine-month hitch', which meant that a man was entitled to his discharge just when he had begun to grasp something of the essentials of his job.

The navy, however, was almost entirely under Federal control, a fact predestined to exert what virtually amounted to a determining influence on the outcome of the forthcoming struggle.

On the southern side the war opened defensively, but for the north the cry of 'On to Richmond!' led to the first battle of Bull Run, of 21 July, 1861, and the complete rout of the Federal forces, a victory which tended to give the Confederates a dangerously low estimate of their opponents' capabilities. It also led the northerners to attach far too great an importance to the defence of Washington, which at the outset became the pivot of their strategy.

By the June of 1863 their

recent victories at Fredericksburg and Chancellorsville had so greatly stimulated the Confederate forces' morale that their Commander-in-Chief, the supremely popular Robert E. Lee, resolved on the bold invasion of northern territory, with the capture of Washington, Baltimore, Harrisburg and Philadelphia as ultimate objectives. For with supplies at their minimum, the Confederate commissary general had bluntly pronounced: 'If General Lee wants rations let him seek them in Pennsylvania.'

In any case success in such a project might well have brought the conflict to a close, while at the same time gaining recognition for the Confederacy on the part of the principal foreign powers.

The Shenandoah valley, guarded by its mountain ridges, formed a fertile corridor to the Cumberland valley of Maryland and Pennsylvania. Running from south-west to north-east, it would bring an invading army closer to Washington with every mile of its advance. So – deliberately risking a counter-stroke on Richmond – it was this route which Lee set out to follow.

Of Lee's subordinate corps commanders General Hill was

General Hooker at Chancellorsville. This victory emboldened the Confederacy to carry the war north. *Opposite*: Confederate generals with Jefferson Davis.

left at Fredericksburg to keep an eye on the Federal general, Joseph Hooker and, together with General J. E. B. Stuart's cavalry, to screen the north-west march of the other two widely separated corps commanded, respectively, by Richard S. Ewell and James Longstreet. Awaiting the opportunity for a stroke against one or other of the divided Confederate forces, the Federal leader, General Joseph Hooker, received orders from the President himself to give priority to measures for the defence of Washington.

By the beginning of the third week in June both the Confederate and the Federal forces were marching on the Potomac, Hooker crossing the river above Washington during the last week in the month. Initially, Lee was quite in the dark as to the Federals' movements and it was only when belated intelligence reached him that his opponents were in full march northwards that he gave orders for his three corps to concentrate for battle. He chose as the point of concentration the town of Gettysburg, a centre near which he hoped to find a suitable battle-ground on which to confront and defeat his foe.

Then, on the first day of July, riding along a road winding through the bright summer countryside, Lee was astonished to be assailed by the harsh sounds of battle – a confrontation he had neither planned nor ordered. In effect, some of his marching columns had butted in to a number of opponents near Gettysburg, and an exchange of shots gave every indication of developing into a major encounter. Withdrawal was still possible, but the so-recently victorious Confederates were in no mood to retire. 'If the enemy is there,' Lee pronounced, 'we must attack him', and he turned a deaf ear to the cautionary comment of his subordinate, James Longstreet: 'If he *is* there, it will be because he is anxious for us to attack him – a good reason, in my judgment, for not doing so.'

In any case considerable time had to be expended by Lee in marshalling his forces. He had momentarily lost touch with his cavalry, but in due course he succeeded in concentrating his 81,000 troops with which to tackle opponents numbering just on 100,000, no longer under the command of Hooker, but of his replacement, General George G. Meade.

Throughout 1 July fighting was desultory and on a limited scale as both sides sought to establish themselves in advantageous positions in and around Gettysburg, with the paradoxical situation of Federal troops advancing from the south and Confederates converging on the township from the north-east, north, and north-west.

Gettysburg itself was sheltered by Seminary Ridge, and it was here that the Union forces took up position. It was here that the ten brigades of the Federal I and XI Corps were attacked in the afternoon by eight brigades that deployed along Willoughby Run. Another five brigades formed a line astride the Mummasburg/Carlisle roads, and a further five brigades formed a line across the Heidlesburg highway.

The Federal troops held their line until Barlow Knoll, on the right flank of the XI Corps, was taken in a brisk assault, whereupon both corps fell back through the town. Closely pursued, they were nonetheless able to form line on the remaining reserve brigade on Cemetery Hill, the Confederate pursuit being halted in the town itself.

On 2 July Lee was urged to move round the left flank of the Union Army to get between it and Washington. But the Confederate commander was confident that he could defeat the Union force as it lay directly in front of him and

Lyon, the Union general, meets his death at Wilson's Creek.

then destroy it in pursuit. After hard fighting, Longstreet enveloped the Federal III Corps and forced it back from its advanced position to Cemetery Ridge.

But the Confederates were unable to effect a lodgment on the Ridge, where all the Union troops were now finally in position, while Ewell's artillery had been overpowered by the Union's admirable counter-battery fire from Cemetery and Culp hills, his infantry assault was also driven back.

By the morning of 3 July both Lee and Meade had concentrated their respective forces on the field of Gettysburg. Lee was confident that victory was still well within his grasp and decided to renew the battle by attacking the Union centre, on Cemetery Ridge, where it approached nearest to the Emmitsburg road, with the divisions commanded by Generals Pickett, Heth, Pender and Anderson. At this point an assault could be enfiladed only by the hostile batteries on the eminence of Little Round Top on the southerners' right flank, and these Lee believed could be silenced by his own artillery.

Lee's army retreating across the Potomac.

After certain preliminary activities on the Federals' right flank, in which Meade's XII Corps attacked a division and two brigades of Confederates posted beyond Rock Creek and drove them back, Lee's main assault force was assembled along Seminary Ridge. Since Lee had failed to effect a permanent lodgment on either of the Federal flanks, and Meade had subsequently thrown up additional field works to harden their defence, all that remained to the Confederate leader was an all-out attempt to break his opponents' centre.

At 1 p.m., therefore, the Confederate artillery opened fire on the Union lines with 138 guns, to which the Federals could reply with no more than 71 pieces. At 1.30 p.m. the Confederate infantry, 15,000 men garnered from four divisions, formed up in long lines to launch their attack on the Union centre. As Longstreet issued his final orders a grim-faced George Pickett hastily scribbed a note to the southern belle to whom he was betrothed: 'If old Peter's [Longstreet's] nod means death, good-bye and God bless you, little one.'

Across the long rise of open ground Lee's 15,000 stalwarts strode at a steady, even pace, the blue flag of Virginia

floating bravely over their serried files. Solid shot, grape and canister tore into the ranks from the Union guns, to be joined by a tempest of rifle fire as the men in grey still thrust their way up the incline.

But the whole morning had been spent by Meade in strengthening his central position. Immediate local command had been entrusted to the reliable Winfield Hancock; additional troops had been allocated to him; batteries were posted on front and flank; at the rear the cavalry were awaiting the moment when a timely charge would turn a temporary check into headlong rout.

Yet despite their thinning ranks the Confederates were still striding valiantly up the slope, and in the teeth of a continuing and withering fire very nearly half of those who had started out reached the Union lines surmounting Cemetery Ridge. It was then that cold steel was put to work, the bayonet, the cut and thrust of the officers' swords, even the clubbed musket, as the men in grey fought desperately to hang on to the battery they had captured and drive their opponents from their position. But it was of no avail; the Confederate ranks had been thinned too shatteringly to hold their momentary gains. As the shrunken lines stumbled back down the slope it was clear that what had been intended for the final stroke had piteously failed.

As the survivors staggered back to Seminary Ridge, Lee rode out to meet them. He was alone, and with the courage of a man brought to despair, he frankly took the blame. 'It was all my fault,' he said, 'now help me do what I can to save what is left.'

Back on the ridge, Lee hastened to make such preparations as were possible to repel the expected counter-stroke. Ammunition was short and so were food supplies; of the Confederate forces 28,000 were killed, wounded or missing.

But with losses totalling 23,000, Meade's army was as desperately in need of reorganisation and reinforcement as that of his opponent. Then, as night closed in on 4 July, heavy rainfall enabled Lee to set out towards the Potomac, with a hesitant Meade making no attempt to harry him in

Gettysburg. The North Carolina regiments attack under General Pickett.

pursuit. In Washington Lincoln groaned in anguish, 'We had them within our grasp. We had only to stretch forth out hands and they were ours. Yet nothing I could say or do could make the Army move. Our Army held them in the hollow of their hand, and they would not close it.'

But there was small need for the president to repine. Even without the follow-up on Lee's reverse, which any General less cautious than Meade would undoubtedly have set in train, Gettysburg – with its heavy drain on irreplaceable southern manpower – was a reverse whose consequences virtually denied reassumption of the initiative on the part of the Confederates for the remaining period of the war.

Moreover, that same day of 4 July had also witnessed the fall of the Confederate stronghold of Vicksburg, which effectively cut off the southerners from all the states west of the Mississippi – an almost illimitable source of supply for cattle, hogs and grain. Thus rejoicings in Washington were as exuberant as faces were understandably downcast in Richmond and throughout the south.

To all intents and purposes the Confederates had shot their bolt. Here and there they struck back with momentary success – as at Brice's Cross Roads and Tupela. But Atlanta

The battle at its height.

fell to the Unionists; the Union Fleet forced its way into Mobile Bay, while Sherman's ruthless 'March to the Sea' scourged the south to its vitals.

Even with the blockade of the southern ports inhibiting the ouflow of essential commerce and cutting off the import even of primary medicaments for the troops, the Confederates still fought on, but rather in fatalistic stoicism than in hope. Sherman, wheeling from Savannah, thrust up through South Carolina, whose northern borders had by then been crossed by Federal troops.

With troops from Grant's command sent westward to overwhelm the Confederates at Five Forks (2 April, 1865), Jefferson Davis fled from Richmond, as the remnant of his battered forces were hustled steadily westwards, the rear-guard ultimately laying down their arms at Sayler's Creek.

Then, on 9 April, at Appomattox Court House, Lee surrendered all that was left of his tattered, half-starving army to Ulysses Grant, the Federal leader carefully emphasizing, 'The war is over; the rebels are our countrymen again; and the best sign of rejoicing after the victory will be to abstain from all demonstrations in the field.'

Gettysburg could scarcely have hoped for a more compassionate epitaph.

SEDAN

On 5 July, 1870, Earl Granville, taking up the post of British foreign secretary, was assured by the permanent head of the Foreign Office that 'in all his experience he had never known so great a lull in foreign affairs'. Unfortunately it was not so much a lull as that dangerous calm which precedes a storm.

For the Europe which had come into being after the defeat of Napoleon and his death in exile in 1821 held out singularly little promise of stability. Characteristically, France had continued to be a bubbling cauldron of unrest. In 1824 Louis XVIII had been succeeded by Charles X, who, in 1830, had been deposed and replaced by Louis Philippe, son of that Philippe Égalité, Duc d'Orleans, who had voted for the execution of Louis XVI. It was also a revolutionary movement which had served to stimulate the passage of the Reform Bill in England, while clearly encouraging Belgium to seek the separation from Holland which was not achieved until 1839.

A brief interval of bourgeois tranquillity ended abruptly in 1848 when once again revolutionary turmoil swept Europe from end to end, with working-class reform movements such

Napoleon III (seated), with his cabinet.

as Chartism rampant in England, and Louis Philippe ignominiously forced to abdicate in France.

In Germany, however, a *Zollverein*, or Customs Union, bound all the thirty-nine Sovereign States in a confederation in which Prussia was clearly destined to take the lead, resentfully as Austria might view the trend.

In 1832, the death of Napoleon's only son, the Duke of Reichstadt, had left Louis Napoleon, offspring of Louis Bonaparte, former King of Holland, as the last repository of the Napoleonic mystique. Although as feverishly ambitious as his uncle had been, his earlier attempts to achieve the throne of France had met with humiliating failure, that of 1840 ending in his condemnation to life imprisonment in the fortress of Ham.

Making his escape from confinement in May 1846, he fled to England, his work of Bonapartist propaganda, *Aux Manes de l'Empereur*, subsequently achieving a considerable clandestine readership throughout France.

It was as the virtual nominee of the Fourth Estate that this Imperial *chevalier d'industrie*, with cynical opportunism, hurried back to France in 1848 to turn the current 'workers' ' revolution to such good account as to secure election to the

Constituent Assembly. Candidature for the presidency led to his election to that office and to his taking the oath of allegiance to a republic whose constitution he proceeded quite shamelessly to dissolve, with the aid of the military, in a *coup d'état* which, twelve months later, enabled him to assume the imperial title of Napoleon III.

Having found a bride in the attractive but ruthlessly ambitious Countess Eugénie de Montijo, Louis Napoleon set out on a career of brazen adventurism which can only be compared with that of 'the Corsican Ogre' before him.

With an eagerly subservient army, a gagged press, and an overawed *bourgeoisie*, the clergy were courted the better to win the support of the peasantry; while, with cynical calculation, the autocrat of the Tuileries proclaimed the peoples' inalienable right to choose their own form of government, a *blague* which enabled France blandly to annexe Nice and the Savoy.

Domestically, the complete remodelling of Paris under the direction of Baron Haussmann enhanced the value of house-property and ensured good industrial wages, while the International Exhibition and treaties of commerce helped to swell the national income. At the outset also a challenging foreign policy, leading to participation in the Crimean War (1854–56), the campaign against Austria in Lombardy (1859), the expedition to China (1857–60), intervention in Syria (1860) and in Mexico (1863), had the support, and in two instances, the actual co-operation, of Great Britain and several other of the powers.

Relations with Prussia and the other German states, however, were on far less even a footing. For example, at the time of the Austrian campaign, following the Gallic victories of Magenta and Solferino, Prussia and her associates had placed their respective forces on a war footing, a broad hint which had distinctly modified the overbearing attitude hitherto taken up by '*l'homme du Kepi*'.

Yet by May 1870 there was again much talk of a Franco-Italo-Austrian alliance against Prussia, although it was all very vague and general, and no one amongst the statesmen and military leaders concerned seemed anxious for immediate and definite commitment.

Then on the first Sunday of June, 1870, a telegram arrived from the French Embassy in Madrid informing M de Grammont that the Spanish Government had offered the country's vacant throne to Prince Leopold of Hohenzollern-Sigmaringen.

Since the last thing Louis Napoleon could tolerate was an obedient client of Prussia beyond the Pyrenees, his protest was immediate and unqualified, his attitude being strongly supported by the French press and public opinion. M Benedetti, the French minister at the court of Berlin, thereupon hastened off to seek the king of Prussia, who was taking the waters at Ems, to lay the formal protest of his government before His Majesty.

On 12 July Prince Leopold made it known that his candidature had been withdrawn. But it was Louis Napoleon's distrustful demand for guarantees that his pretensions would at no time be renewed which brought matters to the point of crisis. At Varzin the Prussian chancellor, Count Otto von

The Montigny *Mitrailleuse* in action.

Bismarck, received a telegram from Ems retailing the story of his sovereign's encounter with the French ambassador, with full details of Benedetti's demand for guarantees, and by a little skilful editing depicted the king's attitude as one of curt and final dismissal of Louis Napoleon's representative.

With the publication of this communication all hope of reaching an accommodation was immediately ruled out by the wildly resentful attitude taken up by the hysterical Paris mob, furious at what it conceived to be a deliberate affront. With the streets ringing with cries of 'To Berlin!' and the bawling of the *Marseillaise*, the war minister, Marshal Leboeuf, having called out the army reserves, solemnly affirmed that 'the chances in a war against Prussia had never been better'.

On 21 July the first shots of the conflict were fired in a skirmish near Saarbruck.

So far as the two countries' respective resources were concerned, von Moltke, King William's chief of staff, had correctly estimated that while he was in a position to put a

Chassepot bullets in manufacture at Lyons.

total of 484,000 men into the field, the most the French would be able to mobilise would be 300,000. In the event, while the German mobilisation was carried out with almost clockwork precision – with the strategic railways built since the instructive American War of Secession more than justifying their considerable cost of construction – the state of affairs in France told a vastly different story. Marshal Leboeuf's vainglorious boast that the French army was prepared for war 'to the last gaiter button' was scarcely borne out by the hopeless confusion over the call-up, which sent one typical reservist – whose movements have been traced – from his home-town in the neighbourhood of Strasbourg, by way of Marseilles, to North Africa. A two-day march then took him to his regiment; he was equipped and given his route back to Strasbourg, where he reported to his field unit after a journey of well over 1,000 miles.

With this example of 'planning', it is scarcely a matter for wonder that railway schedules had not been made out, camps not been pitched because no one knew where to lay hands on the tents. Some formations were entirely without artillery

Above: Bismarck. *Below*: Napoleon III.

support, while others had no transport and still others no ambulances. Moreover, in many instances magazines were found to be unstocked and many fortresses were discovered to be without any reserve of supplies.

The general state of unreadiness for war was scarcely helped by Louis Napoleon's personal assumption of supreme command in the field. Author of a somewhat academic work entitled *Manuel d'Artillerie*, his practical experience in the handling of troops in action was nil. In the opening moves of the campaign this lack of the faculty for practical command became so painfully apparent that the emperor perforce transferred the responsibility to Marshal Bazaine.

The first major French setback was at Saarbrucken on 3 August, and by the 16th the Gallic forces had suffered further defeat at Weissenburg, Spicheren, Worth and Mars-la-Tour. Then on the 18th the Prussian attempt to cut off Marshal Bazaine's withdrawal resulted in the murderous encounter of Gravelotte and the retreat of the French into the fortified city of Metz. Pinned within

Above: von Moltke. *Below*: Bazaine.

its defences were Bazaine and two other marshals, 66 generals, 6,000 officers, and 173,000 rank and file. The investment of Metz, however, removed over a third of the Prussian forces in the field from more active operations. For all that, nothing could now prevent von Moltke from interposing a circle of 250,000 German troops between the only organised army of France and the rest of the country.

With Paris in turmoil, Marshal MacMahon hastened to Chalons, eighty miles south-west of the city of Sedan and on the direct road to Paris, and there hastily improvised a field force which ultimately reached a total of 130,000, with 380 guns. Initially, his plan was to slip to the east around the German flank and effect a juncture with Bazaine at Metz, but this design was frustrated by the 138,000-strong enemy Army of the Meuse with its greatly superior artillery.

By late August MacMahon had pulled his army out of Chalons and concentrated it at Rheims. The march on Stenay, in the hope of linking up with Bazaine, led to a number of minor engagements in which the French were so roughly handled that they were forced to fall back on Sedan.

Thus it came about that on the hills around the city MacMahon drew up his forces. Lebrun commanded the right at Bazeilles; Douay the left at Illy and Floing; Ducrot the centre at Moncelle and Daigny; and de Wimpffen the reserve on the outskirts of the Garenne forest. In effect, the French occupied a rough triangle formed by the Meuse flowing northward, the Floing to the west, and the Gavonne on the east, both emptying diagonally into the Meuse. From the German lookouts their opponents 'lay before them as on a tray', with movement in the streets of Sedan plainly visible.

Lurking unhappily between headquarters and the field works, Louis Napoleon tried to hide the mortal sickness by which he was ravaged by plastering his grey face with a heavy coating of rouge and bravely keeping his saddle, although riding even at a walk was little short of agony.

The morning of 1 September dawned sultry and oppressive with a heavy ground mist. The day started badly for the French, whose outposts had fallen back during the night from their position on the Meuse and from the village of Bazeilles, to which the Prussians promptly pushed forward. In the fighting which ensued Marshal MacMahon was so severely wounded that he relinquished the command to General Ducrot, who immediately gave orders for a general retirement on the plateau of Illy.

But General de Wimpffen was in possession of a letter from the war minister authorizing him, in the event of an emergency, to take over the command. Learning that the French were retiring, he belligerently countermanded the order, vaingloriously assuring a dubious Louis Napoleon: 'Your Majesty need have no fears; within two hours from now we shall have thrust the enemy into the Meuse.' Never can there have been an emptier threat!

In Bazeilles the fighting speedily built up into a major conflict, which inevitably extended to the neighbouring villages of Balan and La Moncelle. With Bazeilles itself a mass of flames, the action spread to the woods of Garenne,

The cemetery of Saint-Privat. A frontal assault on this position caused heavy Prussian losses.

which were simultaneously assailed from the north, the east and the west. As the Prussians thrust home their attack they found 'cannons without wheels, caissons abandoned, a flag whose bearer had been struck down'. Hundreds of men and horses fell into their power, and 'only one French cannon still fired, which was taken when all its team had been put out of action'.

All subordinate engagements, however, were dominated by the general movement on that part of the German Third Army which had been entrusted with the envelopment of the enemy forces in Sedan.

Passing through the defile of St Albert and occupying St Menges, seven battalions began to form front against Illy and were promptly supported by sixty-two guns. A gallant but costly cavalry charge by the Chasseurs d'Afrique failed to check the German crossing of the Fluong tributary in Illy. Gradually the fire of seventy-one batteries – totalling 426 guns – was brought to bear on the Gallic troops enclosed in an ever-tightening cordon.

More and more cavalry charges were launched in the hope of piercing the lines of investment and opening the way for an attack by infantry. One such gallant stroke set out from Sedan's Mézières gate, sweeping through the suburb of Cazal and initially meeting with considerable success. But the alarm once given, the Germans blocked the way with farm carts and carriages, shooting down the cuirassiers as they were pulled up by the impassable obstacles that barred their way.

As the concentric grip of the Prussians tightened one survivor recorded: 'the wrack of the rout is rolling towards the moats of Sedan, which was to swallow up the *débris* of our unfortunate army, consisting of fractions of all corps and all arms. From every point on the horizon shells are being fired which smite the maddened masses in front, in flank and in rear. Amidst shouts of fear mingled with groans, on our right an ambulance bursts into flames and is pulverised by shells. Around us artillery limbers explode, to add to the number of the victims. Everywhere one can see singly or grouped together the riderless horses of the cavalry – exhausted and bleeding.'

French officers surrender.

But in all this confusion and collapse General de Wimpffen's Twelfth Corps had contrived to hold its own. Encouraged by the Bavarians' failure to make progress beyond Bazeilles, its commander determined to call up reinforcements, hurl the enemy into the Meuse, and then cut his way to Carignan. With this resolve in mind, he sent a despatch to the emperor, who was run to earth in Sedan. It read: 'Sire, – I have decided to force the line facing General Lebrun and General Ducrot, rather than be taken prisoner in Sedan. I beg Your Majesty to place yourself in the midst of your soldiers, so that they may have the honour of opening a way for your retreat.'

But Louis Napoleon was no longer in the mood for mock heroics and theatrical gestures. Sedan, ablaze in three places,

A prostrate France at the mercy of Prussia. Contemporary cartoon.

was little more than a shambles. Ducrot, riding into the city, found 'streets, open places and entrances blocked with waggons, carts, cannon and the impedimenta and *débris* of a routed army. Bands of soldiers, without rifles or equipment, rushed here and there seeking refuge in the houses and churches, whilst at the gates of the town they crushed each other to death. Athwart this rabble galloped troopers, their horses with their bellies to the ground, while gunners on their limbers lashed their way through the stampeding mob. Such as were not completely out of their senses had set to work to pillage, whilst others shouted: "We have been betrayed! We have been sold by traitors and cowards!" ' The Emperor had ordered a white flag to be raised over the ramparts, and shortly after had sent a *parlementaire* to offer surrender.

From King William's headquarters at the castle of Bellvue, near Donchery, came acceptance of Louis Napoleon's sword, accompanied by the demand that he name a senior officer 'with full powers to make terms for the capitulation of the army which has fought so bravely under your command'.

At the meeting between Louis Napoleon and Bismarck at Donchery the former was bluntly presented with a demand for surrender all along the line, plus the payment of an indemnity and the cession of Alsace and Lorraine. Whereafter he departed into temporary confinement as a prisoner of war at Wilhelmshöhe.

Meanwhile the unhappy de Wimpffen confronted von Moltke to arrange the submission of all such local forces as survived – 124,000 men, 419 field guns and *mitrailleuses*, 139 garrison guns, 1,172 serviceable vehicles and 6,000 horses.

News of the débâcle at Sedan reached Paris on 4 September, and immediately the streets became clamorous with cries of '*Dechéance!*' and '*à bas Napoleon!*' With Eugénie in flight for England, a Government of National Defence was hastily patched together but it represented no more than a vain attempt to stave off the inevitable.

With the Prussian army advancing relentlessly to lay Paris under siege, Strasbourg surrendered, Orleans was occupied, as was Verdun, while Bazaine's sortie from Metz cost 2,500 casualties and led to the city's inevitable capitulation. By the end of November the enemy's pressure on the capital had attained such strength that a sortie of 90,000 men failed completely to break the hostile cordon by which the city was encompassed.

With the scraped-together Army of the Loire and the scattered forces of the north obviously incapable of coming to the capital's succour, the siege pursued its relentless course. After four months of bombardment and increasingly short commons, nothing was left to the people of Paris but capitulation, with the inevitable sequel of mob violence, the flames of the furtive *petroleuses* and the squalid butchery of the Commune.

The elections of February 1871 created a Third Republic, the first task of whose executive was to sue for terms of peace.

With France obviously prostrated, in the January of 1871, in the Hall of Mirrors at Versailles, William I had been proclaimed emperor of a united Germany. It was a remarkable dividend, on even so far-reaching a victory as Sedan.

THE MARNE 1914

From the formation of the first standing army in 1660 to the Waterloo victory of 1815 the British soldier had found himself in arms against the French in seven consecutive campaigns which altogether embodied over fifty years of hard-fought conflict. It was, therefore, with a certain mild astonishment that 'Tommy Atkins' discovered that the Crimean campaign of 1854 had brought him not only Turkish, Italian and Sardinian allies, but also a considerable body of Frenchmen.

Then with Ferdinand de Lesseps' construction of the Suez Canal and Disraeli's purchase of £4,000,000 worth of shares in the Canal Company, Great Britain and France found themselves in wary co-operation in Egypt. However, during the Arabi rebellion of 1882 and the massacre of Europeans in Alexandria, although a French fleet joined the Royal Navy in the port's blockade, it was left to the British to organize and conduct the campaign which ended with Arabi Pasha's rout at Tel-el-Kebir. The French Government was still afraid of another war with Germany, a dread which the succession in 1888 of the swash-buckling Kaiser Wilhelm II to the Hohenzollern throne did nothing to allay, for a prosperous and expanding Germany was beginning to assert its right to 'a place in the sun' on an equal footing with the existent colonial powers. Moreover, to resentful Teutonic eyes it was clear that the British heir to throne, despite his ultra-Germanic upbringing under the Prince Consort and Baron Stockmar – or as a result of it – was far more Francophile in his sympathies than appreciative of the qualities of a nation whose strutting ruler exhibited little deference for an uncle, seventeen years his senior, who he was delighted to outrank.

Superficially friendly relations between England and France, however, were scarcely improved by the Fashoda incident of 1898. With the British campaign against the Dervishes brought to a successful conclusion by their defeat at Omdurman and the flight of the Khalifa, British forces pressing south in search of him stumbled upon an encampment at Fashoda, on the upper Nile, where the tricolour flying above the post betokened the presence of Major Jean

Baptiste Marchand at the head of a Gallic mission which had left the Congo over two years previously.

The meeting between Marchand and the Sirdar – Sir Herbert Kitchener – was inevitably somewhat abrasive, and Whitehall's subsequent demand for the Frenchman's with-

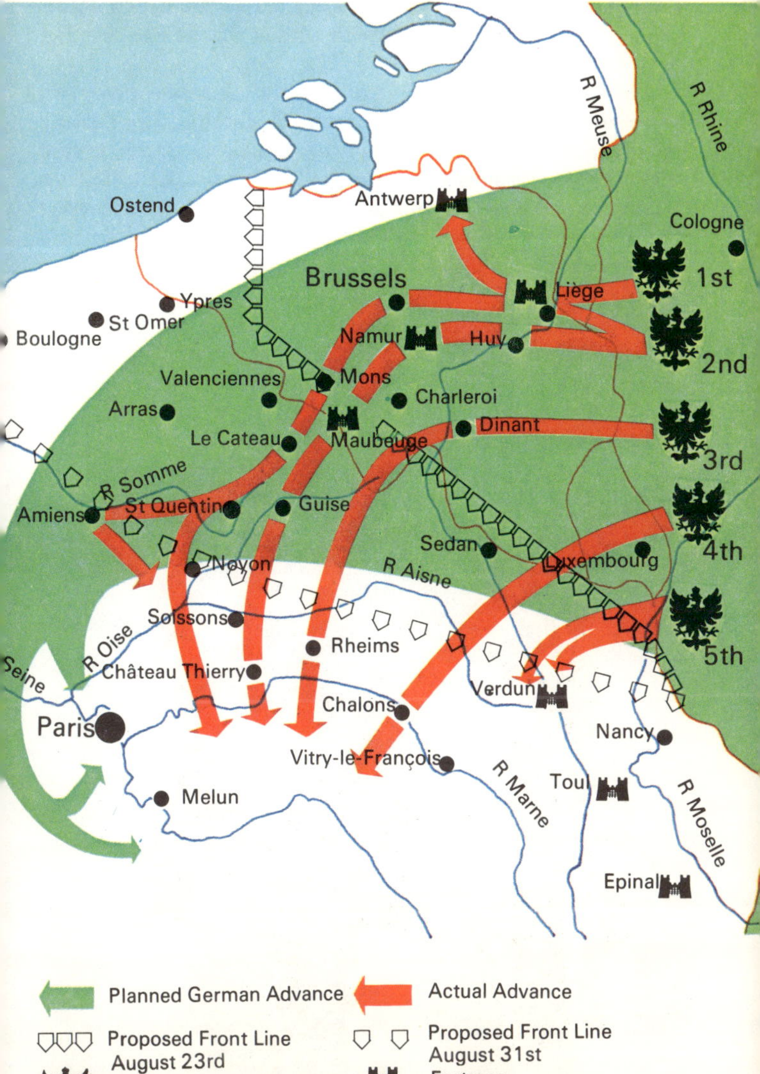

drawal from this 'known sphere of British influence' was greeted with a storm of indignant protest on the part of a France bolstered up by her recent conclusion of a reassuring military treaty with Russia.

Ultimately, however, the French backed down, and whatever plan had been simmering to link up the Gallic territories on the West Coast of Africa with Djibuti on the Red Sea had to be abandoned.

Great Britain's relations with Imperial Germany, however, were not on a noticeably more amicable footing. The Kaiser's telegram to President Kruger at the time of the Jameson raid into the Transvaal had unequivocally congratulated the Boer President on having, by his own 'energetic action', succeeded in 'restoring order against the armed bands that broke into your country.' It followed that the attitude of the German people throughout the South African War of 1899–1902 could scarcely have been more ostentatiously pro-Boer.

On the accession of Edward VII in the January of 1901, if there were little change of attitude where Germany was

German troops build a temporary bridge.

concerned, the hitherto uneasy relationship with France gave place to a considerably more tolerant approach on both sides of the Channel. Carefully fostered by *le roi charmeur*, a growing, if tempered, amicability ultimately found expression in the conclusion of the 1904 *Entente Cordiale*, by whose terms it was agreed that any differences that might arise between the two parties to the compact should be referred to the International Court of Justice at the Hague.

But Russia was still in alliance with France – who had also come to terms with Italy – and Great Britain inevitably went in some apprehension of a Russian invasion of her Indian Empire. Furthermore, the British government was under obligation to go to Japan's assistance were that country to be attacked by more than one belligerent. It therefore demanded considerable diplomacy to steer clear of commitment for or against either power in the Russo-Japanese War of 1904—5.

The next critical situation to arise was in North Africa. Relying on the 1904 agreement with Great Britain, France had adopted a forward policy in Morocco, which in 1905 brought the Kaiser bustling to Tangier to reassure the German Colony that the Sultan occupied an entirely independent position. Strained relations between France and Germany were the outcome, and between 1908 and 1911 the friction increased, with Morocco as the bone of contention.

In 1906, the Balfour Government having been succeeded by an administration headed by Sir Henry Campbell-Bannerman, the Frence cabinet lost no time in high-handedly pointing out that, in the event of a war to which both Britain and France might well find themselves committed, Britain would be in no position to collaborate effectively unless her naval and military leaders had already consulted with the infinitely more knowledgeable Gallic experts. In due course staff consultations were organised in which a number of highly qualified British officers, such as Brigadier Henry Wilson, the future director of military operations and wartime Chief of the Imperial General Staff, feigned to be quite content to sit *in statu pupillaris* at the feet of the patronizing pundits of the French *Ecole Supérieure de Guerre*.

By 1914, with Germany's 1898 Navy Law having resulted in the creation of a fleet strong enough to challenge the Royal Navy, with the German Army steadily increasing in numbers, and with a military mission reorganising the armed forces of an obsequious Turkey, it needed no more than a spark to set the whole continent of Europe ablaze.

A state of war which was speedily to expand into global conflict was precipitated by the assassination of the Archduke Franz Ferdinand of Austria while on a visit to the Serbian city of Sarajevo. Austrian plans to penalize Serbia for the outrage immediately brought Russia to the support of the threatened Slavs, a move which just as promptly evoked a hectoring note from Germany demanding that Russia should cease mobilisation or take the consequences. To this ultimatum the Muscovites returned no answer, and so by 1 August, 1914, Russia and Germany were at war.

The British foreign secretary's plea to submit the dispute

Top left: Galliéni. *Right:* Joffre. *Centre:* Manoury. *Bottom left:* von Bülow. *Right:* von Kluck.

French troops leaving Paris, 1914.

to mediation by the great powers having proved entirely abortive, on 31 July Germany delivered an ultimatum to France calling upon her to surrender her frontier fortresses of Verdun and Toul to German occupation 'as a precautionary measure', following this on 2 August with a demand to Belgium to permit the free passage of German troops.

This definitely violated the Treaty of 1832, by which Prussia, in common with Great Britain, France, Austria and Russia, had solemnly guaranteed Belgium's neutrality. With both Germany's demands rejected, the vanguard of the Kaiser's hordes promptly swept across the Belgian frontier. On 3 August Albert, king of the Belgians, addressed a dignified appeal to Great Britain and announced his firm determination to resist the invaders to the utmost of his power. On the same day Germany declared war on France.

Up to the very last the German government had cherished the illusion that Great Britain would take no positive action.

But there was no delay in the delivery of the British ultimatum, and by midnight on 4 August a state of war had been declared which once again found 'Tommy Atkins' the ally of the *poilu* whose forbears had so often risen in arms against the ancestors of his current confederates.

Because of the need to maintain garrisons in her numerous overseas possessions, the most Great Britain could produce in the way of an immediately available field force was one cavalry and six infantry divisions, totalling some 100,000 officers and men. (Home defence was entrusted to the hastily mobilized Territorial Army.)

Thus by the third week in August the British Expeditionary Force, under the command of Sir John French, had been concentrated in the area Maubeuge-Le Cateau on the left of General Lanrezac's Fifth Army.

The failure of the French Commander-in-Chief, Marshal Joffre, to appreciate fully the strength and impetus of the German advance through Belgium led him to venture an offensive in Alsace and Lorraine, with the result that the French soon found themselves at grips with numerically

Every available vehicle was used to speed the troops to the front.

superior enemy forces on the line of the river Sambre. Meanwhile, at Mons the British troops confronted and successfully held off a more numerous body of opponents by their steadfast refusal to yield to the massive attacks hurled against them. In effect, it was the virtual collapse and scrambling retirement of the French Fifth Army which committed the B.E.F. to that dogged retreat from Mons by which time was afforded their allies to pull themselves together.

To the reasonably discerning it was plain that von Kluck, having swept through Belgium, designed to swing south-west to drive round the western end of the Allied line and interpose his 300,000 troops between Paris and those Franco-British forces which the capital relied on for its defence, for von Moltke's precept of 1870: 'Direction: Paris! Objective: the enemy's field armies!' still governed the German General Staff's thinking forty-four years later.

Reconnaissance by air. A new feature of war.

Thus by 31 August von Kluck's First Army, instead of heading direct for Paris, had swung south-east towards Compiègne in hot pursuit of what he believed to be the routed British and utterly demoralized French. But in doing so he hazardously presented his whole right flank and rear as he bypassed Paris to the Gallic forces under General Gallieni and an entirely new army under General Manoury.

At noon on 5 September a French battery of '75s' debouching from the village of Iverny, something under twenty miles due east of Paris, came under the fire of a German artillery brigade deployed on a range of hills a little further to the east. Badly shaken by the loss of their battery commander, the French gunners beat a hasty retreat, having been the target of the first shots fired in the battle of the Marne.

The general reorganisation of the French forces after their retreat had deployed them on a curved line with one extremity on Verdun and the other on Paris, the central dip reaching almost as far as the Seine. The plan was for Manoury's fresh force emerging from the capital to attack von Kluck's western flank guards and drive them eastwards across the Ourcq river, which runs from the north down into the Marne. Manoury was then to strike at the rear of von Kluck's forces and the adjacent army corps under von Bülow. The task of containing the main mass of the German troops frontally was the responsibility of the B.E.F. and the Fifth French Army, command of which had been taken over by Franchet d'Esperey.

Joffre's original plan of an *attaque à outrance* in Alsace and Lorraine having suffered complete collapse, in the situation by which the Allies now found themselves confronted the British were assigned a similar responsibility to that which Napoleon had allocated to Marshal Grouchy in the Waterloo campaign – to engage and hold von Kluck's forces in their front, while Manoury struck at their flank and rear. At this juncture von Kluck had two corps south of the Marne facing the British, whose line was linked to the left of d'Esperey's Fifth Army by a body of French cavalry.

As developments had worked out, Joffre's battle-area was contained on the left by Paris and on the right by Verdun, and within this arena the decisive conflict would have to be

French infantrymen waiting to cross the Marne.

fought and won. The opening day was 6 September, when, in the early hours, the French Sixth Army, with both its flanks protected by cavalry, moved forward towards the river Ourcq. The heaviest fighting took place on the French right wing. As far as the British were concerned, the struggle was most severe at the village of Barcy – north-east of Meaux – which was taken and retaken three times in an effort to clear the way for the passage of the river Ourcq by the French between Lizy and May-en-Multien.

Since von Kluck had been burdened with the dual task of conforming to the general swing to the east of Paris and at the same time holding off Manoury's Sixth Army, it proved beyond his power to carry out two ex-centric movements adequately with the troops available to him. Moreover, his formations were exhausted by their rapid marches, had suffered heavy casualties and had also seen a number of their components diverted to the defence of East Prussia against the Russians. From the fifty per cent numerical superiority over their opponents which they had initially enjoyed they were now only approximately equal in strength to the Allies on the battlefield. So it is scarcely surprising that a gap of up to thirty miles steadily widened between von Kluck's First Army and von Bülow's Second, an opening only partially closed by a handful of cavalry and a sprinkling of *Jägers* (rifle corps).

Having faced about in conformation with Joffre's re-oriented strategy, the British were now marching directly into the centre of this gap. Their advance was scarcely rapid, however, since they encountered considerable resistance from the stubborn German rearguards.

A typical brush was that which developed with the British move in the direction of Chateau Thierry. An advance guard of the 9th Lancers, thrusting forward into the village of Moncel, found it still occupied by a considerable body of Germans. Without a moments hesitation the leading troop took the village at the gallop and cleared it of their opponents. Very shortly after, however, they themselves were compelled to withdraw, as two fresh squadrons of the enemy's 1st Guard Dragoons bore down on the village from the north. At the same time a third squadron appeared to the west. These new arrivals were promptly charged by a troop and a half of the Lancers, led by Colonel Campbell and Major Beale-Brown. Crashing clean through their opponents, the

German artillerymen with a field gun.

Lancers wheeled to the right to join up with the troop which had already entered the village.

The Germans now retreated to the north side of the cluster of farmhouses and cottages, but in anticipation of this movement a squadron of the British 18th Hussars had already dismounted on that side and were posted among the corn stooks. They promptly opened fire on the Germans, some seventy of whom immediately turned and charged the Hussars in line. With admirable steadiness and nerve, the British let the dragoons get within a hundred yards of them and then practically wiped them out with a single volley.

Such was one of many scores of encounters on a similar or larger scale as the Germans were forced to give ground all along their front and make their way back across the Marne in the general direction of Montmirail. The natural obstacle furnished by three successive river lines – those of the

The Battle of the Marne.

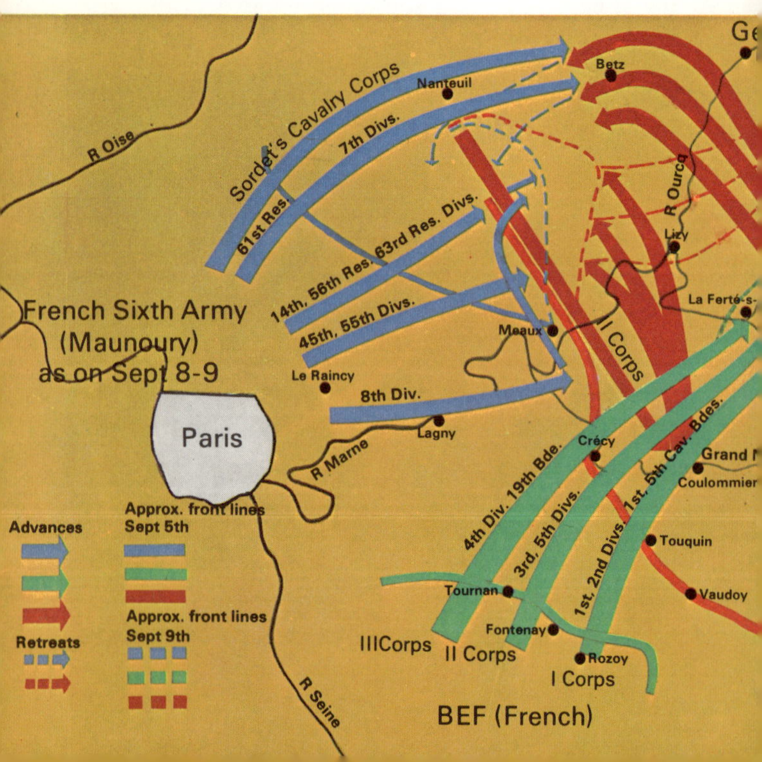

Grand Morin, the Petit Morin and the Marne – and the Allies' struggle to secure their passage, appreciably aided the Germans in slowing down the rate of their opponents' advance. But pressure was steadily maintained, and both the Grand and the Petit Morin were successfully negotiated on 7 September and 8th, while on the 9th the passage of the Marne was forced and the gap between the two German army corps appreciably widened.

By this time both von Kluck and von Bülow were extremely uneasy about the situation developing on their respective fronts. Both therefore 'jumped at the presence of Lieut-Colonel Hentsch, on a vague mission from von Moltke to order retreat if necessary, to get out of a dangerous situation by withdrawing to the Aisne'. The whole German right wing retired behind a hard-fighting rearguard which rendered it extremely difficult for the Allies to get to close quarters. In the outcome the Germans contrived to shake off effective close pursuit and stood to fight again on an immensely

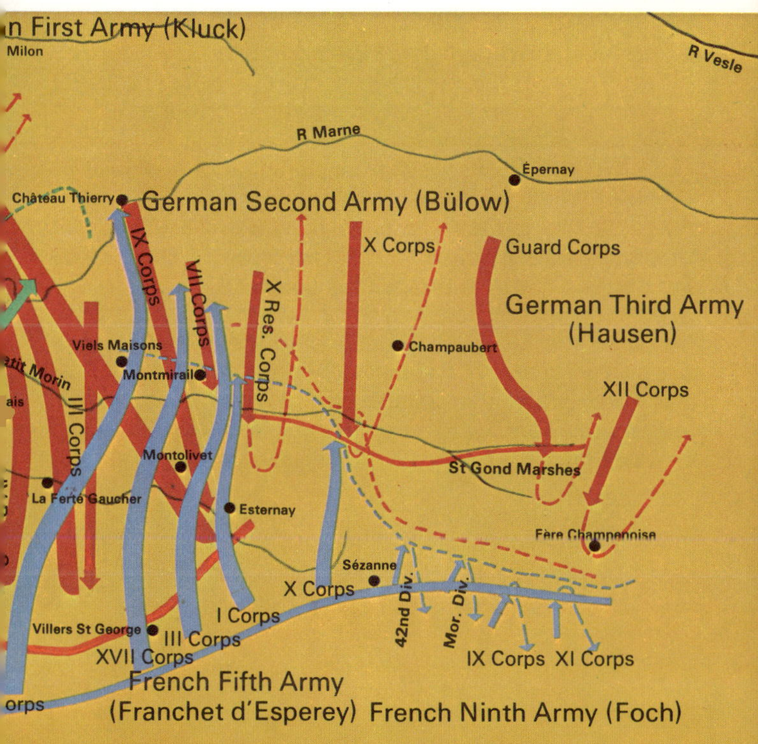

German prisoners after the battle.

strong natural position on the heights overlooking the valley of the Aisne, a position which called for four years of hard fighting before its defenders could be driven from it.

Thus the battle of the Marne came to an end – a German check but scarcely an Allied triumph. But at least it could be claimed that the great German offensive plan to strike down France in the first few weeks of the war had been soundly frustrated. Paris had been spared and it was considered safe for the government to return from Bordeaux.

For all that, it was only too starkly apparent that, in the long-run only a colossal effort by Great Britain could turn the scale in favour of the Entente. In due course that effort was made, but to gain time for it to develop involved little less than the sacrifice of the British regular army – a demand to which the centuries had, unfortunately, only too painfully accustomed it.

Their shoulders held the sky suspended;
They stood, and earth's foundations stay.
What God abandoned, these defended,
And saved the sum of things for pay.

THE NORMANDY LANDINGS, 1944

The Armistice of 11 November 1918 that terminated the worldwide conflict which had been raging since the August of 1914 also brought to an end the Hohenzollern dynasty. With the Kaiser and his heir both seeking political asylum in neutral Holland, post-war Germany adopted an uneasy form of republican government which, by 1925, could discover no more suitable nominee for the role of President than the somewhat deflated war hero Field Marshal von Hindenburg.

It was in a certain erstwhile battalion runner and subsequent house painter named Adolf Hitler that a faltering Germany found her *bierkeller* messiah; whose powers of persuasive mob-oratory soon led to his leadership of the National Socialist movement (*Nazi*), whose aim was to restore the Fatherland to that position of power and prestige it had enjoyed in the heyday of the Hohenzollerns.

Organizing a semi-military body of followers, known as

Tedder, Eisenhower and Montgomery.

the *Sturmabteilung*, Hitler attempted a *coup d'état* in Bavaria in 1923. Its failure led to a short period of imprisonment; but on his release the movement was so carefully fostered and popularized that it rapidly gained ground; its creed of anti-Semitism, anti-Marxism and intense Germanic nationalism finding widespread favour amongst a people desirous of exorcising the sense of defeat under which they laboured.

Gaining the Chancellorship early in 1933, Hitler – having ensured the support of the Italian dictator Benito Mussolini – was at particular pains to cultivate the confidence of the surviving military element; surreptitiously recreating a *Grosse Generalstab* and brazenly repudiating many of the militarily restrictive clauses embodied in the Treaty of Versailles. Growing bolder, on 16 March 1935 he announced the reintroduction of conscription; on 7 March 1936 he reoccupied the Rhineland; on 13 March 1938 he annexed Austria; in the October of the same year he seized the Sudeten areas of Czechoslovakia, taking over the whole of the country on 13 March 1939. Less than a week later he voiced a demand that Danzig should be returned to the German *Reich*.

Patently, the moment for a united effort to call a halt to this cumulative programme of aggrandisment had been with Hitler's re-occupation of the Rhineland in March 1936. For at that juncture the German Army had been no more than half-manned and half-trained; while both the Poles and the Czechs had been ready to march if only France had given the word.

But with Leon Blum's defeatist Popular Front Administration in office and the Baldwin government all too content with the Council of the League of Nations' purely academic condemnation of Germany, it is perfectly comprehensible that the *Führer* should have experienced no qualms in continuing to follow his audacious course.

It was the rape of Poland which precipitated world conflict, since, as Prime Minister Chamberlain publicly affirmed, both Britain and France were under pledge to 'lend the Polish Government all support in their power'. War was declared on 3 September 1939.

Since it is the invariable habit of British governments in time of peace to run down their armed forces far below safety level, it follows that when first committed to action the ut-

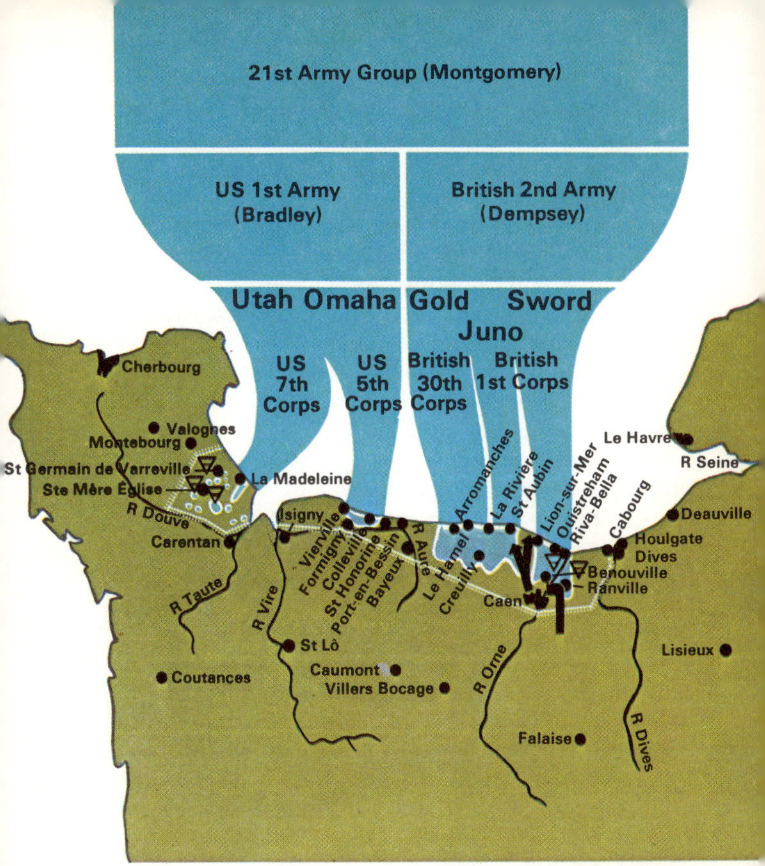

21st Army Group (Montgomery)

US 1st Army (Bradley)

British 2nd Army (Dempsey)

Utah Omaha Gold Sword

Juno

US 7th Corps

US 5th Corps

British 30th Corps

British 1st Corps

Cherbourg

Valognes

Montebourg

St Germain de Varreville

Ste Mère Église

La Madeleine

R Douve

Carentan

Isigny

Vierville

Formigny

Colleville

St Honorine

Port-en-Bessin

Bayeux

R Aure

Le Hamel

Creully

Arromanches

La Riviere

St Aubin

Lion-sur-Mer

Ouistreham

Riva-Bella

Le Havre

R Seine

Cabourg

Deauville

Houlgate

Dives

Benouville

Ranville

Caen

R Taute

R Vire

St Lô

Coutances

Caumont

Villers Bocage

R Orne

Lisieux

Falaise

R Dives

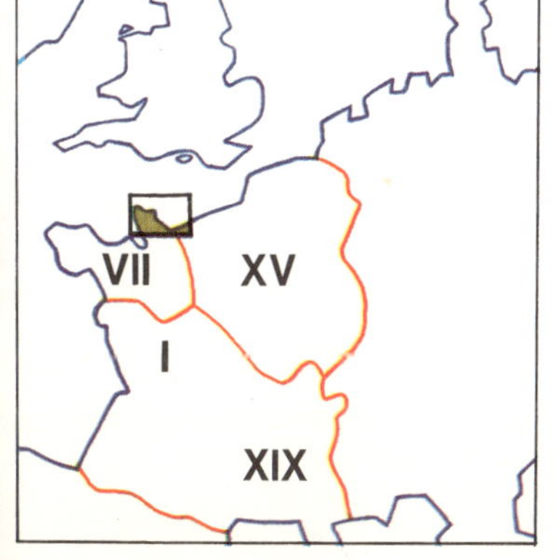

XXI Panzer Division's afternoon counter-attack

Airborne landing zones

Area Allies held at 2400 on D-Day

Planned Allied beach-head at 2400 on D-Day

Sword Assault beaches

The D-Day Plan.

Inset: Area occupied by German Armies on 6 June 1944

most gallantry cannot spare them the initial disaster their want of numbers brings down upon them. Thus when Hitler followed his conquest of Poland and Norway and his subjection of Holland and Belgium by a *blitzkrieg* against the Anglo-French forces deployed along the Dutch, Belgian and Luxemburg frontiers, a gap was speedily created between them they were entirely unable to close. Fighting a stubborn rearguard action the British Expeditionary Force was slowly forced back upon and ultimately evacuated from Dunkirk; while of Marshal Pétain's far more numerous forces Admiral Leahy, the American observer attached to them, acidly commented, 'All I know of the "magnificent French Army" is that it was dam' fast on its feet.'

Britain's Royal Air Force, in the hard-fought Battle of Britain, denied any hostile landing force the air cover essential to such an enterprise.

Throughout the rest of 1940 Britain's strategy remained primarily defensive: to keep her sea-lanes open, to blockade the coasts of German-held Europe, and to bomb the enemy war plants as vigorously as possible. During the course of 1941, however, help was sent to the Greeks to try and stave off invasion; successful campaigns were undertaken in Abyssinia, Iraq and Syria; while preparations were put in hand to organize an expeditionary force to check the Germans' Italian allies in North Africa's Western Desert.

It was in the June of 1941 that Hitler committed the fundamental error of abrogating his non-aggression pact with Russia by launching a foolhardy invasion of the country which no belligerent has yet succeeded in penetrating to his advantage. In December of that same year, Hitler's Japanese allies ensured the entry of the United States into the world conflict by their wanton bombing of the Hawaiian naval base at Pearl Harbour.

With Allied efforts in 1942 and 1943 bringing victory in North Africa; with the capture of Sicily leading to the penetration and imminent subjection of Italy, and with the counter-offensive against Japan steadily progressing, the Anglo-American authorities were free to concentrate on the ultimate objective – the invasion of German-held Europe. Clearly, the best way to defeat Hitler's *Reich* was by a con-

American assault craft.

certed attack on the vital, highly industrialized Ruhr Valley, a stroke which necessarily involved a prior triphibious assault on a reasonably accessible part of the European coastline. This meant that the most suitable assault base would be found on the southern coastline of England.

Certain that in due course he would have to contend with a large-scale invasion attempt, Hitler organized a defensive *Festung Europa* (European Fortress) which ran for over two thousand miles, from Spain's Atlantic border-line along the Channel shore of France to Amsterdam. Even with the Russians to cope with in the east, defence of this 'Atlantic Wall' demanded a minimum of 25 static coast divisions plus 16 field-force and parachute formations. Control of these was entrusted to Field Marshal von Runstedt, with Erwin Rommel, of Western Desert fame, commanding the 7th and

15th Armies which were responsible for covering the coast from Holland to the river Loire.

Command of the steadily assembling invasion force was allocated to General Eisenhower of the United States, with General Montgomery as his leading field commander. Air Chief Marshal Leigh Malory was to be responsible for air operations and Admiral Sir Bertram Ramsay for all naval activities. Air Marshal Tedder acted as Deputy Supreme Commander.

As a preliminary, the crippling of German means of reinforcing and resupplying their forces defending the Atlantic Wall had been put in hand in ample time for them to achieve maximum effect. Railway marshalling yards, repair depots, dams and bridges had been bombed into ruin, as had *Luftwaffe* reserve centres and workshops.

In due course, D-Day – the day on which the invasion would be launched – was provisionally fixed for the early June of 1944, when it could be anticipated that weather conditions would be at their most propitious. All through the

Flying Fortresses of the Army Air Corps.

earlier months of the year the preparations, put in hand as early as 1942, began to build up on such a scale that by late spring British, American and Allied forces had been assembled whose total came to 3,469,000. For the transport of their spearhead across the narrow seas to the chosen invasion zone on the Cotentin peninsula 4,000 assault craft had been assembled, plus 1,600 merchant ships and ancillaries; with 1,200 Royal Navy vessels, of all classes, to act as guardians and to support the actual invasion attempt with their fire.

The air component, apart from training machines and replacements, consisted of 13,000 aircraft and 3,500 gliders.

As the month of May drew to a close tension at Eisenhower's headquarters at Southwick House, outside Portsmouth, steadily mounted. The great question was would the weather hold for the scheduled 4 June D-Day landing on the chosen beaches and for the transfer of the reinforcements and supplies that subsequently would have to be set ashore?

On 26 May the assault troops had been moved forward to the marshalling areas near the ports of embarkation, where they were sealed off in fenced-in camps to undergo a

thorough briefing on the task which lay ahead. By 3 June thousands of troops had been consigned to their landing craft, awaiting the word that would set the whole stupendous venture in motion.

In the interim elaborate measures had been taken to delude the Germans into the belief that the invasion attempt would be made in the Pas de Calais area. Dummy landing and support craft filled Dover and the neighbouring havens as far as Sheppey and the Isle of Grain. Vast camps were simulated; empty or non-operation airfields sprouted aircraft and gliders made of plywood; rubber tanks and guns were ostentatiously encamped in the open. In Zurich, Stockholm and Madrid suave British Embassy officials guilefully made 'guarded' enquiries for copies of the Michelin mapsheet No. 51 – which covers the area Calais-Boulogne.

As finally determined, the extreme limits of the actual assault area were defined as extending from Caen, on the east to Quinéville, some fifty miles to the west.

The strategic plan was that the Americans should land on the right, or western half of the battle front, with the ultimate objective of securing Cherbourg for use as an entry port for reinforcements and supplies. The British were to be set ashore on the eastern flank, with the immediate objective of securing the line St Mère Eglise – Carentin -- Bayeux – Caen; the last-named being a useful port linked by canal to the sea.

To precede the landings an elaborate bombing operation had been organized not only to blast the German ground defences, but to put out of action as many aircraft and enemy airfields as concentrated effort could contrive to immobilize. At the same time a hoax operation was organized with the intention of deluding the Germans into the belief that the real assault was to be made in the area Boulogne–Calais – a ruse which certainly plunged both von Runstedt and Rommel into considerable confusion.

To confound the enemy further the experts of the Royal Navy's and Bomber Command's counter-measures section had succeeding in distracting, obfuscating and bluffing the enemy radar watchers to the point where they could give no reliable

Landing, and first casualties.

warning as to where the actual invasion attempt was likely to take place.

At Command Headquarters, however, meteorological forecasts were so unpropitious that all idea of launching the enterprise on 4 June, as had originally been intended, had to be abandoned. It was not, indeed, until 4.15 a.m. on the morning of 6 June that, with the weather showing slight improvement, General Eisenhower gave the laconic order, 'O.K., let her rip!'

Thus as daylight strengthened, with 117 minesweepers ploughing ahead to clear the course, an armada made up of 6 battleships, 23 cruisers, 104 destroyers, 4,102 landing craft crammed with troops, 315 coastal and 152 escort vessels, 4 monitors, 324 auxiliary craft, 224 merchant ships and 1,032 small 'tramps' and blockships, thrust steadily forward across the Channel waters. Scores of motor torpedo boats and motor launches stood by to serve as navigational guides or to lay

American assault troops landing on D-Day.

smoke screens; while others guarded the armada's flanks against possible assault by E-boats out of Le Havre, or by the seventy-six U-boats known to have been concentrated in the Biscay ports.

Ahead of the beach landings an air-drop by the British 6th and American 82nd and 101st Divisions had been planned with the object of protecting the flanks of the main assault force. This in its turn was preceded by an air-drop of a large number of dummies, dressed in parachutists' uniform and fitted with fireworks timed to go off at intervals, to represent rifle and gunfire. At the same time Allied bombers dropped large quantities of foil strips, a proven method of confusing hostile radar observers, which had the effect of deluding them into the belief that the dummy parachute attacks were at least twenty times bigger than in fact they were.

With the actual air-drop, although the British Division was landed precisely on its objective, the Americans were badly scattered over a fifteen by twenty-five mile area of the Carentin region; a misfortune which had serious reper-

cussions on the progress of the United States' forces set ashore on their designated landing areas.

A patrol of 29 British Lancaster bombers then swept in to jam the enemy radar services on a scale hitherto unmatched throughout the whole of the war.

With the massed gunfire of the Royal Navy pouring its missiles into the Atlantic Wall at the rate of two hundred tons of shells a minute, the landing craft began their final run-in over a choppy sea, heading for their respective beaches. These were named *Juno, Gold* and *Sword* for the British and Canadians on the left flank, *Omaha* and *Utah* for the Americans on the right. Meanwhile Boston bombers of the 2nd Tactical Air Force's No. 2 Group laid down two immense smoke screens to obscure the operation's flanks and veil the assault craft from such coastal guns as might still be able to fire.

As the landing-craft approached closer to the shore, a total of 1,077 Fortress and Liberator aircraft dropped 3,096 tons of bombs on the German defences covering the beaches; the smoke-clouds arising therefrom helped materially to obscure the assault troops as they came dripping up on the foreshore. So well-ordered had been the planning and so speedily were the beach officers put ashore from the landing craft, that they were in position to mark the boundaries of the landing areas, so that at approximately every seventy-five yards a landing craft touched down at the precise place assigned to it in the overall plan.

Particularly good fortune attended the landing of the British 6th Division, for example, which got ashore to seize useful bridgeheads east of the Orne river. They were materially aided in the destruction of defensive devices by the use of tank-flails and armoured bull-dozers; the rejection of which by the Americans came to be greatly regretted.

The troop landings were also greatly helped by the covering fire furnished by a number of amphibious tanks, which followed closely on the heels of the landing craft to give their occupants the closest possible support. Although of the thirty-two D.D. (Duplex-Drive) tanks launched six miles out to sea only five escaped foundering, in the main the amphibians succeeded in getting ashore to render the

A tank fitted with a mine-blowing device.

infantry full support. In addition, and immediately available were assault engineer tanks, tank-carried bridges for crossing anti-tank ditches, mat-laying tanks for covering soft sand patches on the beach, and ramp-tanks over which other tanks could scale sea walls.

Additional support was also given by rocket ships, firing over the heads of the troops to explode the mines on the beaches and rend apart the thickly-meshed barbed wire.

Nonetheless the first waves ashore came under extremely heavy fire; the Americans suffering particularly severely since the losses in D.D. amphibians denied them the steady fire with which their own 'deep-water' tanks supported the British landings.

In the outcome, having recovered from the stunning impact of the penultimate bombardment, the German coastal troops put up a thoroughly determined resistance, which subjected the first waves of the landing parties to a steady stream of vicious machine gun, mortar and rifle fire. But as

reinforcements poured ashore, on all the beaches save *Omaha* the Germans were driven from their frontline defences.

Thus as D-Day progressed, the fifty miles of Normandy coastline containing the five beaches passed steadily into the invaders' possession; with the two artificial 'Mulberry' harbours – each as big as Dover harbour – being towed into place and safely secured. Once in position they speedily proved their value in the transfer of stores and heavy equipment too weighty for landing craft to handle. As the enemy was driven further inland, bulldozers hacked roads up from the beaches, while trucks rolled off the landing ramps to carry their loads to rapidly growing supply dumps.

Caen and some of the other villages of the peninsula demanded hard fighting for their capture; and Cherbourg called for a major operation to bring it to submission. But Admiral Ramsay was indulging in no empty boast when, eight hours after the operation's start, he confidently affirmed; 'We have broken the crust and started off on the proper foot. Now we must try not to give him [the enemy] a chance to regain his balance. We've got through the defended beach zone. We have made it possible for Montgomery to fight a land battle . . . We have not gone in to hold a bridgehead. God forbid! We must advance. The crust is broken, and now we must go through it . . .'

In effect, by sound planning and sheer hard fighting the Allies, for losses not exceeding 11,000, had secured the initiative; the road to Paris, the Rhine and beyond, lay ahead.

As in Africa and in the Pacific, the Normandy landings had given overwhelming proof that a dominant sea-power still retained its traditional advantage of being able to strike virtually where it elected and thus exploit the priceless element of choice to its fullest advantage.

Well planned and admirably fought, D-Day 1944 clearly falls into the category of 'one of those few battles of which a contrary outcome would have essentially varied the drama of the world in all its subsequent scenes'.

In the outcome it is scarcely to be denied that *paritur pax bello* – that, in the ultimate, peace is the blesséd outcome of war.

German prisoners.

BOOKS TO READ

Aron, Raymond *The Century of Total War*
Barker, W. Alan *The Civil War in America*
Beatson, Henry *Memoirs of Great Britain* (6 vols)
Burne, Lt. Col. A. H. *The Art of War on Land*
Catton, Bruce *The Coming Fury*
Coblentz, S. A. *From Arrow to Atom bomb*
Coxe, William *Memoirs of the Duke of Marlborough* (3 vols)
Doyle, A. Conan *The British Campaign in France and Flanders*
Eisenhower Foundation *D-Day*
Falls, Cyril *Great Military Battles*
Fortescue, Sir John *History of the British Army* (13 vols)
Freeman, E. A. *History of the Norman Conquest*
Fuller, Major-General J. F. C. *Armament and History · The Second World War*
Guedalla, Philip *The Second Empire · The Hundred Days*
Hamley, Sir E. B. *The Operations of War*
Hargreaves, Reginald *The Bloodybacks*
Hudleston, Frank *Gentleman Johnny Burgoyne*
Lloyd, E. M. *A Review of the History of Infantry*
Oman, Sir Charles *A History of the Art of War*
Parkman, Francis *Half a Century of Conflict*
Platt, Washington *National Character in Action*
Preston, A.; Wise, Sidney F.; Werner, Herman O. *Men in Arms*
Savage, J. *The Turkish History*
Vagts, Alfred *A History of Militarism*

The sources for the quotations in the text are as follows. 'Blenheim': *Letters and Despatches of the Duke of Marlborough* by General Sir George Murray; Fortescue (see above). 'Quebec': PRO Colonial Papers; *George Washington* by Michael de la Bédoyere; *Montcalm and Wolfe* by Francis Parkman (also see above); Hargreaves (see above). 'Saratoga': PRO Colonial Papers; Hudleston, Fortescue and Hargreaves (see above).

INDEX

Page numbers in bold type refer to illustrations.